Teach As He Taught

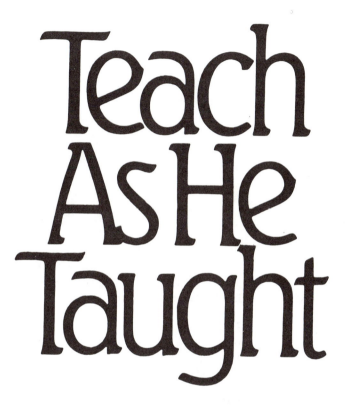

Teach As He Taught

Robert G. Delnay

MOODY PRESS
CHICAGO

Library of Congress Cataloging in Publication Data

Delnay, Robert G., 1926-
    Teach as he taught.

    1. Christian education—Teaching methods.   2. Jesus Christ—Teaching methods.   I. Title.
BV1534.D37   1987   268'.6   86-23845
                      ISBN: 0-8024-4340-0

1 2 3 4 5 6 7 Printing/LC/Year 91 90 89 88 87

Printed in the United States of America

To June,
for her constant encouragement
and her consistent example
as an academic

Contents

Introduction

We often teach about Jesus. We teach the gospels. We teach the Old Testament prophecies. We teach His second coming, His virgin birth, His miracles, His absolute truth, and His offices of Prophet, Priest, and King. We teach His redemptive work from both Testaments. We teach His presence in the believer and hold to the validity of the Great Commission. Almost incidentally we know that He was and is the greatest teacher. Since He is not just Lord and Redeemer but also Teacher, this book will attempt to apply His methods to our teaching and bridge that ministry to our own experience.

We must begin by accepting the fact that we will have limitations. We cannot do everything that He did. We do not have supernatural knowledge or perfect wisdom. Many of us purport to be Bible expositors, yet we have nothing like His total, intuitive knowledge of the Bible. We may review all our memory verses, pull out all our outlines, review all our notes, and we will still fall short of His ability to perceive the best way to handle every situation. Paul said we have the mind of Christ and the blessed Spirit indwells us, yet we must admit that our grasp of the Word is at best sketchy compared to His. All His utterances were in harmony with divine truth, and we may believe that He never broke that perfect consistency. Who of us could come near that claim?

Jesus showed perfect knowledge of the human heart (John 2:23-25), a discernment we yearn to have. As we read the gospel accounts we realize that He never misjudged a person. Could we not wish that we had never been taken in by flattery? That we had never come down too hard on the truly penitent? That we had never too quickly excused the unrepentant? That we had never mistrusted an honest person or trusted the faithless? Whatever reasons Jesus had to include Judas with the twelve, we can be sure that He was neither deceived nor surprised by his character. Jesus had a perfect and intuitive knowledge of human nature, and His life was a constant expression of that knowledge.

Jesus transcended another limitation: our concern for numbers. After feeding the five thousand (John 6), Jesus had a crowd following Him. Yet He deliberately repelled them, first by exposing their materialism, then by using difficult language and making astounding claims, culminating with verse 53: "Except ye eat the flesh of the Son of man, and drink his blood, ye have no life in you." That was too much for the crowd. In less than an hour they went from adulation to grumbling. Jesus asked, "Doth this offend you?" and He added three more statements, at least as crushing as any He had yet uttered. That did it. As the numbers departed, He stood with the twelve. "Will ye also go away?"

Would you or I ever do that? Apart from our fear of alienating people, who of us would have the discernment to grasp the situation? Who of us has the words just strong enough to repel the carnal and still keep the serious with us? Even apart from the supernatural elements in Jesus' handling of that situation, few of us could come close to carrying it off.

We can learn from Christ our Teacher, but from the outset we know that some of the rules that applied to Him do not apply to us. We teach with that limitation.

We must also accept the fact that we use many teaching practices that are outside Jesus' pattern. We need to admit those differences, use those that are helpful, and be prepared to discard those that are not. Jesus is the friend of sinners, but He is no great friend to human traditions.

A first obvious difference is our penchant for organizing schools. We have generally committed ourselves to the idea of college or university as the final step in a person's formal training. Jesus did teach in synagogues (Mark 6:2), but He seems never to have come even close to our commitment to formal schools.

What about teaching in church? Clearly, Jesus founded the church (Matthew 16:18-19), but by most of our understandings He never taught in one. Sunday school classes? They may come closest to reflecting the style Jesus used to proclaim the message of the cross. But remember that Sunday schools as we know them trace back only a little more than a century. Let us admit that our schools are our own inventions, and let us walk softly.

What else do we do that Jesus did not? We believe in a clearly stated curriculum. Jesus gave us no formal statement of a curriculum. He had one (John 17:8), but He gave us no outlined formulation of it. Indeed, He hardly wrote at all, so far as we know.

We make grateful use of our technology and of the many teaching devices now at hand. Jesus used no technology. His visual aids were simple—no slides, no overhead projector, no video, no copy machine—not even a chalkboard.

We give written assignments. His exams were oral and informal or else carefully arranged to test the disciples' faith. We are forever making lists and outlines, but He never enumerated a list of more than two items (Matthew 22:39-40).

We put a great deal of stress on Bible teaching, and rightly so (2 Timothy 3:15—4:5). Yet the only clear mention that Jesus taught Bible is in the record of the two disciples on the Emmaus road (Luke 24). We might suppose that He taught Old Testament to His disciples, but the gospels record hardly a word to indicate that He did.

We pray with our students. For all that the gospels tell us, He never did. He prayed for His disciples, even in their presence (compare Luke 6:12, Luke 11:1, John 17, and Matthew 26:36-45). He taught them to pray in Luke 11, and several times He commanded them to pray. In the garden He told them to pray while He prayed, but He did not pray with them.

We quote all sorts of human authorities. And since we cannot match His distinctive authority, we must constantly precede our teaching with phrases such as, "This verse probably means . . ." Jesus never had a doubt. The prophets said, "Thus saith the Lord," but Jesus' formula was "Verily I say unto you." We assert things saying, "In my judgment," or, "It seems to me," or, "In my own opinion." Even as we make those assertions, there is something tentative about them. Jesus did not qualify His statements the way we must qualify ours.

We must spend time in preparation. Although Jesus, as we suppose, could lecture impromptu, organizing in a moment, we ourselves do not often have it come that way. We take whatever training we can get. We collect books until we run out of shelf space. We have to spend time at the desk, and, having spent it, we realize that He prayed more and studied less—or not at all. We may pattern our lectures after His, but His mind created the molecules, the genetic code, the galaxies, and we find ourselves toiling over periodicals and making preliminary outlines on scratch paper.

After excluding all the disparities, what is left for us to apply? A great deal, and all of it is in the four gospels. We cannot perform the supernatural, but we can still learn to teach as He taught.

Getting Ready to Teach

In all things shewing thyself a pattern of good works.
—Titus 2:7

But be thou an example of the believers, in word, in conversation, in charity, in spirit, in faith, in purity.
—1 Timothy 4:12

If our preparation for teaching is to be anything like that of Jesus, it will involve a lifetime. We need to support our teaching with lives that command respect if we are to accredit what we say. Jesus commanded the respect of His hearers. Some may have hated and envied Him, but they knew that He was genuine. People may oppose our teachings, but if we are faithful and sincere, they will recognize that.

Where does lifetime preparation begin?

Knowing God

Jesus prayed, "And this is life eternal, that they might know thee the only true God, and Jesus Christ, whom thou has sent" (John 17:3). He was saying that salvation itself is a matter of being acquainted with God.

Jesus also spoke of His own acquaintance with the Father (John 7:29; 8:55; 10:15; 17:25). How did He maintain

that acquaintance? Primarily through His prayer life.
Some sixteen or seventeen times the gospels mention that
He prayed, sometimes briefly, sometimes for whole nights.
Matthew 17:21 implies that He had the habit of spending
much time in prayer.

How do we get acquainted with the Father? The same
way—by spending time with Him. Both Scripture and experience tell us that we should spend time each day with
God. Our meeting should be unhurried, a time in which
we give Him our undivided attention in worship, confession, Bible study, and supplication. We must expect difficulty in keeping the appointment, "for the flesh lusteth
against the spirit" (Galatians 5:17). Yet the earnest believer
will thirst after that communion. Let us hope to meet Him
because we joyously want Him. Some mornings we may
wake up weary or depressed and have our devotions from
a sense of duty. But whatever our motives, our faithfulness
will be rewarded. We owe it to our students to spend time
with Him every day.

Our time should include Bible study. Each of us has
his own practice, whether it means following the readings
of a devotional guide, reading the Bible through in a year
or more, or reading the Bible consecutively. Reading a
chapter a day will take us through the Bible in a little more
than three years. But whatever our custom, if we love God
we will love His Word; we will esteem it above our necessary food (Job 23:12).

In the last year I counseled two Christian workers
whose ministries had failed. I asked each one, "How has
your quiet time been lately?" Each answered, "Well, that's
been a problem"—meaning no daily devotions in more
time than he cared to admit. One of them even got defen-
sive. He thought he had spent a lot of time on his teaching
preparations and that people owed it to him to listen with
respect. Neither of the two understood that if he did not
meet God in the morning, he could hardly hope that God
would see him through his ministry that day.

If we attempt to teach without first meeting God, we

may still find ways to impress the students, but we will not impress God. On the other hand, if we have come to know the sweetness of time with Him, we can hope that at least some of our students will come to find that same sweetness alone with God. If so, they will come to it not because we lectured it to them, but because we lived it.

KNOWING THE BIBLE

A second step in lifetime preparation is knowing the Bible. Jesus' knowledge of Scripture was total and intuitive (John 3:11; 7:15). Our knowledge doesn't come that way; we know in part. We probably have a residue of Bible knowledge to draw on, verses and facts that we have been learning ever since we were saved. But in addition to those, we need a life of ongoing Bible study. That means that we should both study and teach the Bible. We should set aside particular times each week for personal Bible study, perhaps as part of our daily quiet time. We should memorize verses and paragraphs of Scripture, and we should find ways to review what we have already hidden away. We should check our knowledge of various books of the Bible by reviewing from memory the leading idea of each chapter.

In addition to those obvious uses of our Bibles, we should collect the tools of intensive Bible study. A complete concordance such as *Young's* or *Strong's* opens the door to the original languages, resources into which any Bible student can tap. If you want to sight-read Hebrew, you're going to need two or three years of classroom study; to read the Greek testament, you're going to need a year or two. Short of those amounts of time, the grammar and the verbs will remain mysteries. However, word studies are another matter. You can get access to those by memorizing the alphabets. In two hours you can memorize the Hebrew alphabet, and in about an hour you can learn the Greek. With that knowledge a person can make fairly intelligent use of the lexicons, the books of synonyms, the word studies, and even such specialized works as Hebrew and Greek concordances.

If that idea intrigues you, you might want to start with Edward W. Goodrick's *Do It Yourself Hebrew and Greek*. It can advise you on which tools to buy and show you how to use them.

ENDURING TESTING

Integrity of character requires testing. Jesus' ministry began with testing. Mark used a strong word in describing that: "the Spirit *cast* him out into the desert" (Mark 1:12, emphasis added; author's trans.). In the desert Jesus learned suffering, in this case the voluntary self-denial of nearly six weeks of fasting. Then the devil came and tried to tempt Him to sin. Jesus faced essentially three temptations at the beginning of His ministry, and all resulted in victories over Satan. The night before Calvary He would say to the eleven, "Ye are they which have continued with me in my temptations" (Luke 22:28). It would seem that despite His original victory over the devil, the testings returned all through those years. Those testings, like many of ours, came in the path of obedience.

We may yearn for Jesus' record of victories, but most of us live with Peter's track record. We will face testings that come in three classes. The first is the appeal to the body and its demands: "Command these stones to become bread" (Matthew 4:3). For Daniel, not even being a eunuch protected him from the lust of the flesh, and he purposed in his heart that he would not defile himself with the king's food.

The second test is the appeal to the eyes. Satan offered Jesus all the kingdoms of the earth in exchange for one momentary concession: that Christ bow down to him. To us the test may come in various forms, each offering something enticing to the eyes and bidding us to ignore Scripture. That involves a level of self-denial and rigorous control of our innate covetousness and curiosity. "If thine eye offend thee, pluck it out" (Matthew 18:9). If we agree that the Bible does not teach mutilation of the body, it at least does command us to deny ourselves ruthlessly, and it offers the hope of victory through the Word.

The third test is the one that seems to get less pulpit coverage: the temptation to pride. To Jesus the test was the impulse to put on a spectacular event. "Cast yourself off the edge; the angels will help you, and you will amaze the crowd" (Matthew 4:6), Satan implied. Well, how does a person work miracles humbly? Yet Jesus worked countless miracles and healings and never succumbed to pride. Legend has it that the following conversation took place in Spurgeon's tabernacle after a service:

"Sir, that was the greatest sermon you ever preached."

"Yes, I know."

"You—know?"

"Yes. The devil told me the same thing just a few moments ago."

Students have a right to expect trustworthy teachers. Jesus resisted temptation by using Scripture. Frail as we are, we are under obligation to qualify ourselves by walking softly, by confessing sins and keeping short accounts with God, by pleading before the throne for a measure of victory, and by bearing the fruit of the Spirit. Jesus said that others would know us by our fruits. If our students do not see love, joy, peace, longsuffering, and the rest of the character of Christ in us, they have the God-given right to pronounce us phonies.

No wonder James warns us, "My brethren, be not many masters [teachers], knowing that we shall receive the greater condemnation" (James 3:1).

DEVELOPING ZEAL

"The zeal of thine house hath eaten me up" (John 2:17).

Near the outset of Jesus' ministry, just before the Passover, He went up from Galilee to Jerusalem. John records that Jesus went up to the Temple and with whip and force of character drove out the merchants. The disciples then recalled the Old Testament verse that speaks of the zeal of God's house (Psalm 69:9).

While the example of that event is not necessarily something we should imitate, it does suggest a further qualification we need if we are to teach. Jesus burned with zeal for the work to which the Father had called Him. In recent days, the teaching zeal sometimes seems to be growing dim. If God has called us to teach, we need to examine our hearts to see how much passion we have for the truths we teach. If we do not have some fire in our bones, we should question whether we are ready to follow our Lord into a teaching ministry.

What if we just do not have much zeal? We would do well to examine ourselves, asking:

1. How much do I love the Bible?
2. How much do I stand in awe of God?
3. How much gratitude do I have that Jesus died for all my sins?
4. How deeply am I convinced of the reality of hell?
5. For the truth of what I believe, how much group pressure am I prepared to resist?
6. How much has it cost me to serve Christ, saying no to the flesh? How much have I done for Him that my flesh did not want to do?

Love means purposing the good of another, at any cost to oneself, hoping for nothing. "We love him because he first loved us" (1 John 4:19).

How does a believer remedy a lack of zeal? It is a matter of (1) earnest confession of sin and (2) time spent with Him. We can get as close to Him as we want, and we have the promise, "Him that cometh to me I will in no wise cast out" (John 6:37).

THE GOALS OF TEACHING

Why do we teach? What makes us tick—or at least —what *should* make us tick?

In Jesus' case, teaching was a holy compulsion as well as a life work. Luke 4:18-19 says that the Spirit was upon Him, that He was anointed to proclaim the gospel to the poor. Those around Him perceived Him to be a teacher. The gospels mention forty-five occasions that He taught, but they mention only thirteen times that He preached. Forty-six times they called Him Teacher, fifteen times they called Him Rabbi, but not once did they call Him Preacher. Teaching was His primary ministry.

But why do we teach? We can point to various legitimate motivations that go with pleasing and glorifying God. We get real satisfaction from discovering biblical truth and sharing it with our classes. We get even greater satisfaction from seeing our students walking with God, and we rejoice to see God reproducing Christ in them.

If those compulsions and satisfactions make us teach, what goals do we then pursue in our teaching?

TEACHING GROUPS

Jesus' first goal was to instruct the crowds. He chiefly lectured to the crowds, first offering them the kingdom and then preparing them spiritually for it. Along with preparing them for the kingdom He gave them eternal principles of knowing God.

So how do we work toward that goal? By teaching the Word to larger groups even if we concentrate most of our energies on training disciples. We need to teach groups wherever we can find them, and we need to plan our curriculum from Jesus' fundamental teachings.

PLANNING CURRICULUM

Jesus prayed, "I have given unto them the words which thou gavest me; and they have received them" (John

17:8). That verse implies that Jesus had a distinct body of truth to convey to His own. As we try to summarize that body of truth, we can condense it into about five areas that we ourselves need to cover:

Jesus Himself. Jesus opened His ministry by preaching that the kingdom was about to come. He did not need to describe the kingdom, because the prophets had already described it. By implication He was offering Himself as the rightful King and Messiah. Early on He made the momentous claims that John records in chapters 5-8. Because Jesus claimed to be deity, the Jews threatened to stone Him. By other testimonies, however, Jesus revealed His supernatural power and knowledge, His deity and His humanity. When Peter makes his great confession in Matthew 16, Jesus tells him to keep quiet. But now we do not keep it quiet. We need to teach about Jesus Himself.

Spiritual life in the world. Jesus taught at length that heaven's values are the reverse of the world's values. He began His teaching with the Beatitudes, which by the world's pragmatic standard are nonsense. Jesus continued throughout His ministry to emphasize that contrast. We live in this world, but our citizenship is in heaven. If our treasures are there, our teaching will reflect that. If we teach others to lead a spiritual life, we must teach at least these principles:

First, we must teach others about the new birth. Jesus taught a radical view of conversion—not just a prayer, but a pivotal decision in a person's life; not just some fresh resolves, but a new life. The believer has not only Adam's life, but God's life imparted through the Holy Spirit (John 3:3-8). We are both created and begotten. You probably have had the experience of talking with a person who is devoid of interest in spiritual things, ignores the Bible, never prays, takes a casual view of the cross, yet claims to be born again. He is miles away from what Jesus taught.

Second, we must teach internal religion as opposed to

external. In Jesus' time, Judaism had come to the point of all established religions: its demands required only outward performance, not a change of heart. Its devotees could satisfy all the demands of their religion and still envy, hate, resent, or have outbursts of rage.

We deal with the same mind-set today. We will meet some professed believers, devoid of discernment, who love the world and the things that are in the world. On the other hand are those who separate themselves from the world but have cold hearts toward Christ and His own. If we would follow Jesus' curriculum, we must teach a heart-thirst for Him, a thirst that yearns for heaven, visits the fatherless, and keeps itself unspotted from the world.

Third, we must teach about the world's hatred. All through Matthew 8 and 9 Jesus faces rising opposition. In turn He warns His disciples of the world's hatred, beginning with His warnings in Matthew 10 and finishing in John 15: "Because ye are not of the world . . . therefore the world hateth you." We must teach the need for radical conversions and then warn people that they shouldn't expect their old friends to congratulate them for loving Jesus and following Him.

Fourth, we must teach the plan of redemption. While the disciples were hardly ready to grasp it, Jesus taught the death principle, that He would give His life a ransom for many. They did not understand until later, but those teachings gave them the basis for what later became the developed doctrines in the epistles, notably Romans 5:8, 1 Peter 2:24, and Hebrews 9-10.

Fifth, we must teach about the ministry of the Holy Spirit. Like the plan of redemption, this also was too hard for the disciples to understand. Since holiness could come only to the redeemed, it could come only through the enabling of the Comforter.

The claims of devotion. A third aspect of Jesus' curriculum dealt with the cost of devotion. The flesh prefers a religion that makes light claims, but Jesus confronted us with an infinite love and holiness that makes absolute claims. Repeatedly He invited men to follow Him. Repeatedly He warned them of the costs of following: "If any man will come after me, let him deny himself, and take up his cross daily, and follow me" (Luke 9:23).

The postponement of the kingdom. A fourth aspect of Jesus' curriculum was that He was not going to establish the kingdom right away. True, He had honestly offered it at the beginning of His ministry, but Israel found the price too high. Instead of repenting of their sins, Israel's leaders began plotting to kill their Messiah (Matthew 12:14). In our ministries, we teach that Jesus is coming back to reign but that in this present age God is testing us by making us wait for His return.

Missionary work. Finally, the last area in Jesus' curriculum comes close to our idea of "skills." He taught the inner group how to do missionary work. He first showed them by His example how to preach and minister (Matthew 4-9). He then instructed them and sent them out (Matthew 10; Mark 6:7-13; Luke 9:1-6). I leave it to you to translate His training into your own teaching, so that you put your own disciples to work preaching and teaching what you have taught them. This hands-on experience becomes an important part of reaching our next goal.

TRAINING DISCIPLES

At the same time that Jesus was ministering to groups, He carried on a parallel ministry to His disciples. We need to carry on that second ministry to our disciples. We need to concentrate our attention on those few to make leaders of them. If concentrating our attention can be called favoritism, then our Lord Himself was guilty of favoritism. He concentrated on the twelve, and He took only the inner three to see Jairus's daughter raised, to climb the mount of transfiguration, and to pray near Him in the Garden.

As we concentrate our attention, our general aim is to make disciples, people who purpose to live and die for Christ. We should not so much cover material or teach measurable skills as we should build character. In the building process, however, we will teach a great deal.

CONCLUSION

Why then do we teach? We teach primarily because we know that God has drawn us into that ministry. We may get certain satisfactions from our teaching, but they only put sunshine on the path. The satisfactions do not determine the path.

We need to teach with divine objectives. We are promoting a small but world-wide movement by making disciples, seeing them baptized, and instructing them; we rest on Jesus' presence and power until the end of the age. In the narrowest sense, we are imparting Jesus Christ and Him crucified.

Questions for Discussion

1. To what extent do the fruits mentioned in Galatians 5:22-23 explain what Jesus meant when He said that by their fruits ye shall know them? Why not by their works? Why not by their gifts?
2. Is it wrong to teach for the sheer joy of teaching?
3. To what extent is it the church's duty to train leaders? If our tradition favors a school-educated ministry, how valid are our reasons for that tradition?
4. As Jesus taught the crowds, what statements of purpose can we formulate for His teaching?
5. How do we set about to impart to our students the skills of Christian service?

2

The Lecture Method

And he opened his mouth, and taught them.
—Matthew 5:2

To some of us, teaching is lecturing and lecturing is teaching. Everything else is either preparation or distraction. The student who raises his hand to ask a question annoys the lecturer and interrupts the teaching process. The student who takes notes and reviews them is the finished product of the lecturer's art. The lecture has the advantage of conveying information and opinion to a large number of people at one time. We have, from Sunday school to graduate school, built much of our educational system on lecturing.

We may sometimes have misgivings about the effectiveness of this method. We think that a certain lecture got across. If we then follow it up with a test, what do we find? How much did the students get out of that lecture? How much did they write in their notes? How precise were their notes? How much was lodged in their memory? How much could they explain back to us? How well did they understand the content of it? How well could they apply that understanding in problems only indirectly related to our subject?

You may have heard a student say something like, "I

know I failed that course, but I got a lot out of it." How do you respond to *that* remark?

With most of us, even at our best, our lectures leak —and sometimes badly.

Jesus lectured; therefore, there must be something good about the lecture method. We believe that He did it right, and we want to believe that there is a way that we can do it right.

The gospels record some twenty-five or thirty extended discourses. How many of those can we call lectures? If a lecture is an extended, formal discourse to instruct, then a good half of those discourses fit the description. They give us examples from which we can draw general principles. The discourses that last more than six verses running, or that give an extended series of statements interrupted by the crowd, may be listed as follows:

1. The Sermon on the Mount (Matthew 5-7)
2. The similar material in Luke 6:17-49
3. The messages to His disciples on how to evangelize (Matthew 10; Mark 6:7-11; Luke 10:2-16)
4. The discourse to the crowd concerning John the Baptist (Matthew 11:7-24, 27-30; Luke 7:24-35)
5. The answer to the Pharisees' accusation (Matthew 12:25-45; Luke 11:14-28)
6. The discourse on the kingdom program (Matthew 13)
7. The discourse on His own nature (John 5:19-47)
8. The Bread of Life discourse (John 6:26-65)
9. The discourse in the Pharisee's house (Luke 11:37-50)
10. The warning against things (Luke 12)
11. The warning against traditions (Matthew 15:3-11; Mark 7:6-15)
12. The discourse on the Sabbath (Luke 14:8-24)
13. The costs of discipleship (Luke 14:26-35)
14. The discourse on the Father's heart (Luke 15)
15. The discourse on coveting (Luke 16:1-13, 15-31)

16. The discourse at the Temple (John 7)
17. The light of the world (John 8:12-58)
18. The Good Shepherd (John 9:41—10:18) and the aftermath at the Temple (10:25-38)
19. The discourse on the child (Matthew 18:1-35)
20. The condemnations of the priests and elders (Matthew 21:28—22:14; Mark 12:1-11; Luke 20:9-19)
21. The woes on the Pharisees (Matthew 23)
22-23. The discourses on the end times (Luke 17:22-37; Matthew 24-25; Mark 13:2-36; Luke 21:5-36)
24. A further discourse on the end times (John 12:23-36, 44-50)
25. The Last Supper (Matthew 26:21-35; Mark 14:18-31; Luke 22:15-38; John 13-16)
26. The Emmaus road exposition (Luke 24:25-27, 33)

If a lecture is an extended, formal discourse to instruct, some of these passages particularly invite us to study them as lectures: Matthew 5-7, Luke 6, Matthew 10, Luke 12, John 5, and Matthew 24-25. In addition, compare those with Matthew 13, Luke 15, and Matthew 21:28—22:14. We have to believe that Jesus lectured superbly. What then can we learn from Him to help our own lectures?

GETTING THE INFORMATION

At some points He gives us little to imitate. For example, how did He prepare? By Him were all things created. If He created the billion visible stars in our galaxy in a day or in a moment, did He need any time to collect the material for the remarks He was going to make? The mind that on the sixth day created man with sixty-five thousand protein molecules in every cell would not need long to prepare the Sermon on the Mount or the Olivet discourse.

Jesus simply *knows*. We know in part, and most of what we learn comes hard. I will not labor the point; those of us who teach know the sweet satisfaction that comes when we know the material. We may also remember the pain of facing a class without having mastered the material. The beginning of wisdom is the fear of the Lord, and the beginning of our teaching is research.

We have long since learned that we have to have the proper material. That means collecting, checking, correcting, and reflecting on material until we are satisfied that we have something to teach.

PUTTING IT TOGETHER

Once we have the material, we have to organize it into bite-sized chunks. We need it in a form that we can understand and that our students can understand.

Note how Jesus organized the teachings in Matthew 5-7. His central idea, His theme, had to do with being right with God. The following outline shows His organization.

Introduction: The Beatitudes, heaven's reversal of earth's values. "Except your righteousness exceed. . ."
 I. The Heart of the Law (5:22-48). "Ye have heard . . . but I say unto you."
 II. Worship from Within (6:1-18)—Alms, prayer, and fasting
III. God Before Things (6:19-34)
 IV. The Christ-Life in Contrast (7:1-27)

Another example is the Olivet Discourse (Matthew 24-25). It can be outlined as follows:

Introduction: The apostles' questions: When? What sign?
 I. Future Events (Matthew 24)
  1. The end of the age (4-14)
  2. The Great Tribulation (15-26)
  3. The second coming (27-31)
 Applications (32-51)

II. Events Related to Christ's Return (Matthew 25)
1. Surviving Israel, ready and not (1-13)
2. Reckoning with the servants (14-30)
3. The surviving Gentile nations (31-46)

Exercise: We have an extended discourse in Luke 12. Assume its unity, and try to establish its theme. Spiritual genuineness (v. 1)? True wealth (v. 15)? Some other phrasing? Now mark the transitions in the chapter, and see if you can label the main divisions in it.

Jesus used a second kind of lecture that seems to have consisted almost wholly of illustrations. Matthew 13:34 appears to say that every time Jesus taught the crowds, He gave them parables. Sometimes the whole lecture may have been a series of illustrations (for examples consider Matthew 13; Luke 15; Matthew 21:28—22:14).

Why parables? The first of those three examples seems to have been used to arouse their curiosity and to intrigue some of them to come closer and ask for more truth. And note the words "the kingdom of heaven is like." Jesus was not describing the nature of the kingdom, since the prophets had already gone to great lengths to describe it. He was answering the question, What has to happen so that we can have the kingdom?

Note that in verses 10 and 36 the disciples converge on Him to get more. Jesus then gave them more and explained three parables in such a way that they might be able to figure out the others. Note also that even while teaching in parables, He organized His material. Each passage shows progression.

The other two examples of lectures in parables are cases of instructing His enemies. In Luke 15 Jesus speaks "this parable" to a cold bunch of beady-eyed critics. They had charged, "This man receiveth sinners and eateth with them" (v. 2). The parable then comes in three forms: the lost sheep, the lost coin, and the lost son. But the focus of the chapter is not so much on the lost object as on the joyful finder, and, in the parable of the lost son, the older brother. We wonder if the Pharisees got the point. For all the sermons we hear on the prodigal son, how many do we hear on being in sympathy with the heart of the loving Father?

Exercise: In Matthew 21:22, Jesus is in tense confrontation with the religious establishment—men who are already plotting His death. List the probable reasons that Jesus uses illustrations rather than explanations in this setting. In what sorts of situations can you use this approach? What progression can you find in this discourse?

WEIGHING ITS URGENCY

It is worth taking time to review the topics on which Jesus lectured. Some topics that are now making reputations and fortunes, He apparently skipped. How could He have missed the possibilities in the importance of a good self-image? How could He say so little about family living, or about personal fulfillment, or about how to succeed in the business world? Why did He ignore the wonderful vitality you can get from vitamins? You can think of many reasons, but they all boil down to this: He had more important things to lecture about.

As we settle on our own topics, we exclude others. We need holy wisdom to know what to skip and more wisdom to keep covering what is biblically, doctrinally, and spiritually urgent. Paul wanted love to produce discernment in his readers, so that they could test the values that differ (Philippians 1:9-10). If that applies to moral choices, it also applies to teaching choices. In the twenty-six long discourses listed above, about one verse in three involves prediction. That suggests that we have reason to teach about the future and to urge that concern on our disciples. He repeatedly condemned externalism and taught a radical conversion. Though He neglected religious pop psychology, He had much to say about discipleship.

THINKING IT OVER

Did Jesus need to ripen His lectures by taking time to reflect on them? It's unlikely. In contrast, most of us would agree that our lecture plan is never really finished. Till the moment we walk before the group our minds are still spinning off fresh insights, no matter how thorough our preparation before that moment. In fact, the more we prepare, the more we can expect fresh insights to come after we have finished the lesson plan.

The director of duplicating in one school was fond of saying, "There is no reason a teacher can't plan ahead and do his handouts three days in advance." Perhaps. But then, he had never been a teacher. He had his fingernails on the truth, though. If a lecture does not have time to marinate, don't expect it to be well seasoned. Your mind needs time to meditate, and the advance work makes the meditation possible. But don't be surprised if the night before class you revise your handout.

TEACHING WITH AUTHORITY

"And it came to pass when Jesus had ended these sayings, the people were astonished at his doctrine: For he taught them as one having authority, and not as the scribes" (Matthew 7:28-29).

Do we have a way to get that kind of authority? His authority is inherent and intrinsic; ours is derived. A man has nothing except what is given him from heaven. In our teaching we can get at least some authority from above. We use our minds to master our subject, and just as Jesus taught with absolute expertise, we can achieve a relative expertise based on study.

Second, we can base everything possible on the Word of God. Where Jesus said, "I say unto you," we can say, "The Word of God says." Our own words may not be quick or powerful, but His words are absolutely living and powerful. That is why we memorize verses and study the Bible. As an old professor said about collateral reading, "Something sticks," and he pointed to his head. As we study the Bible, something sticks and gives us material to draw on when we lecture.

We can teach with authority when we can assure ourselves that we are conveying the truth as precisely as we can.

INVOLVING OUR HEARERS

Jesus spoke to His hearers in a way that concerned them. In Matthew 5 alone (KJV*), you will find some ninety second-person pronouns. Many of us prefer to say "we," because saying "you" makes us feel as if we are pressing a forefinger into a student's eye. If on the other hand you study Matthew 5, you will find ways to teach in terms of your disciples' experience and interests:

> Blessed are ye (v. 11).

> Ye are the salt of the earth (v. 13).

> Ye are the light of the world (v. 14).

> Ye have heard (v. 21).

> If then you are offering your gift on the altar and there recall that your brother has something against you, leave your gift there in front of the altar and get going; first make it right with your brother, and then come and offer your gift (vv. 23-24; author's trans.).

If we want our lecture to grip people, we have to put it in terms of their interests and feelings. We use such words as,

> "How do you feel when someone. . ."
> "Think of this in terms of your own experience."
> "Try to put yourself in Job's place."

*King James Version.

"Have you known what it is to pray for something when God seems to be putting you off?"

"Now, you have read the book of Ecclesiastes. . . ."

Involving our hearers should be more than just a useful device to help people listen. It should come from a sincere concern for other people. If we have that concern, it will show in our lecturing. If we want to lecture the way that Jesus did, we will not merely pronounce truths in the presence of our disciples.

CHARITY

Some teachers flatly forbid questions during their lectures. Others accept questions grudgingly and give curt answers. To them any question is a threat and becomes an act of hostility, so they fight back, and they rarely forget. Still other teachers accept questions because they provide them a chance to show their knowledge and wit—or a chance to humiliate any student so dumb as to ask a question.

The gospels tell us of many questions and other interruptions while Jesus spoke. Some of those came in scorn (note the nine times that happened in John 8:13-57). John 8 is a study in how to answer opposition, even heckling. If we want to follow Jesus' way of taking hostile interruptions, we will hold our tempers, we will keep in mind the sincere ones in the crowd (8:31-32), we may answer sternly but not sarcastically, and we will guard our dignity. May these confrontations be few. What of all the rest?

Jesus answered with charity and patience. Note the exchanges in John 14:

> And whither I go ye know, and the way ye know.
> Thomas saith unto him, Lord, we know not whither thou goest; and how can we know the way?
> Jesus saith unto him, I am the way, the truth, and the life: no man cometh unto the Father, but by me. If ye had known me, ye should have known my Father

also: and from henceforth ye know him, and have seen him.

Philip saith unto him, Lord, shew us the Father, and it sufficeth us.

Jesus saith unto him, Have I been so long time with you, and yet hast thou not known me, Philip? He that hath seen me hath seen the Father. (John 14:4-9)

Jesus spoke without impatience, put-downs, or digression. He gave straight and kind answers. If we love our students it should not be hard to be kind to them. But even when they try our patience, we must remember that if we ever humiliate a student, we lose him—and most of the class—and we may forfeit our chance to teach him anything. Only a frank apology before the class can restore our moral credit.

Jesus answered with wisdom, sometimes turning an interruption to His purpose. In Luke 12 He is lecturing on spiritual reality, of the danger in honesty, and on the coming ministry of the Holy Spirit. At that point one of the listeners cut in; he probably hadn't heard a word that Jesus said. He had a problem: his brother was not treating him fairly. Would the Righteous One please straighten things out?

In this case Jesus begged off. "Man, who made me a judge or a divider over you?" (v. 14). Then He seized the subject and the occasion to instruct both the man and the whole crowd: "Take heed, and beware of covetousness: for a man's life consisteth not in the abundance of things which he possesseth" (v. 15). He then launched into a story with which every middle-aged man could in some way identify: the story of the man who decided to retire and live for himself. Jesus used the interruption as a way to lead into the next part of His lecture.

But what about us? What do we do when someone asks a question, and we just don't have the answer? Simple. We admit that we don't know. If we believe the question merits it, we can write it down and try to have the answer the next time. But no bluffing; it carries too many hidden charges.

Consider this incident from a New Testament class of the late J. R. Mantey, coauthor of the widely used *Manual Grammar of the Greek New Testament.* A student was explaining how the graveclothes had collapsed in such a way as to prove Jesus' supernatural resurrection. Mantey remarked, "Why, I never saw that before!" A number of men in that class mentioned afterward how their respect for Mantey had soared after that childlike admission.

Do we ever have reason to ignore a question? In Luke 12 Jesus seems to do just that. He was telling His disciples to be like those who wait for their Lord to return from the wedding. Possibly He had already given intimations of a rapture and a wedding before His glorious return. But was Jesus saying that the saints of the coming age would be on earth when Christ comes back in glory to set up His kingdom? The question bothered Peter. He asked, "Lord, speakest thou this parable unto us, or even to all?" (Luke 12:41). Jesus ignored Peter's question and went right on talking: "Who then is that faithful and wise steward, whom his lord shall make ruler over his household?"

Luke did not record any sign that may have passed between the two. So how do we apply that in our teaching? For one thing, Jesus had already answered the question in verse 36: "And ye yourselves like unto men that wait." It also appears that the Lord did not want to digress into eschatology. There was time enough for the Holy Spirit to cover that later. Jesus' purpose was to warn and exhort His disciples to be in constant readiness for His return.

We know that some questions hinder the teaching process. When the wrong question comes up, or the talker speaks at the wrong time, we do what we assume happened in this instance: smile at the student in such a way that promises an answer later and go right on lecturing.

MAKING IT CLEAR

Jesus tried to be clear. If expositors do not come up with identical interpretations of His discourses, we know that it is not from any fault in His teaching method but differences in the expositors. To read His discourses gives the impression that He wanted to be clear. When scholars try to interpret the discourses literally, they come out remarkably close in their understanding of what He taught. We need to admit that our traditions and preconceptions bear on every line we read. If we can find a way to put some distance between ourselves and our traditions, we may be able to evaluate the discourses in the light of Scripture. Our payoff will be twofold: some of our traditions will now find a biblical foundation, and the rest will probably go overboard—and just as well. Jesus wanted to be clear, and as we question our traditions we have our best chance to learn what He meant.

To lecture clearly, it helps to set your purpose. Determine to make your students understand. Think about how many lecturers merely pronounce information in the presence of their classes. Then think about how many lecturers teach in order to impress, to fill the time, or to cover material. Although tons of educational texts deal with the affective and cognitive aspects of the learning experience, in practice little of that teaching turns up in adult Sunday school classes or in higher education. The beginning of clarity comes in the teacher's determination that his people understand, not that he just cover the material.

A second step to clarity is thinking it through. Just as we need to reflect on the lecture outline for completeness and freshness, we need to think it through for clarity. The idea that seems so marvelously clear to us often puzzles or baffles the friend we explain it to. How can you help him understand? On the lecture platform, it is probably too late. If we rephrase the matter often enough, sooner or later it will get across. But what lecture outline do we have that we could not improve by just reflecting on it? We must often ask, How can I make this fresh and vivid? How can I make it clear?

Robert Hawkins, missionary to Latin America, once told of the problems he and his two brothers had in making the gospel clear to a remote tribe. By the time they had a grasp of the language of the Wai Wai, they learned that the tribe had no concept of comparison, no word for "like." Any time one of them tried to illustrate a Bible truth by using an analogy, tribal elders would shout, "Liar! liar!"

The three of them went into seclusion. For a week of intense concentration they thought and argued through the first eight chapters of the book of Romans until they could each explain every paragraph of it—without using a single comparison or analogy. Hawkins described that as the most demanding mental challenge of his life—and that comment from a man who had already learned Portuguese and at least one unwritten tribal language.

A third step toward clarity is in our choice of words. What can we gather from Jesus' vocabulary? The disciples heard Him in Aramaic (e.g., Mark 5:41) and recorded His words in Greek. Most of us read in an English translation. But anyone who deals with another language, such as a missionary or one who signs for the deaf, knows that Jesus' words are marvelously translatable. There is a reason for that. Study His words, and see how many abstract words you can find.

Even in teaching about the unknown, He used words we could feel: "Let not your heart be troubled: ye believe in God, believe also in me. In my Father's house are many mansions: if it were not so, I would have told you. I go to prepare a place for you. And if I go and prepare a place for you, I will come again, and receive you unto myself; that where I am, there ye may be also" (John 14:1-3).

In English, not one word goes more than two syllables. Even in Greek, with all its inflections, only twelve words in this passage go more than two syllables. Do we want to teach clearly when we lecture? We will pay attention to the vocabulary we use, to keep it both simple and exact, to explain every technical word we need to use, and to use our words with consistency.

What else do we need to do to make our lectures clear? A key matter is the one that the Wai Wais could not bear: comparisons. Some of those are brief analogies and metaphors, as, "For as the lightning cometh out of the east, and shineth even unto the west, so shall the coming of the Son of man be." Some are whole stories. Where is the use of illustration any more important than in our lectures?

CONCLUSION

There has to be a way to lecture well; Jesus did it well. We can compile our information and put it into logical order. Then we can find the ways to make it clear and memorable. Having done that, we can work within the limits of the method. For example, the lecture is not the best way to convey masses of data, although verbal dictation is one way to transfer data from our notes to our students' notes. When we have textbooks and duplicators, however, we can better use those devices for the data and use our lectures for other kinds of information.

Jesus succeeded with His lectures. How can we know when our teaching succeeds? We need feedback from our students to determine their understanding. If the feedback shows that they understood the lecture, well and good. If they did not understand, let us remember who their teacher was. If a student fails our exam, it may very well be his own fault. If the class fails, it was really the teacher who failed it. Our duty is to make the students understand.

A graduate student asked his teacher, "Doc, do I gather that nine of us out of seventeen flunked that last exam?"

"I believe that's right."

"That's pretty heavy, isn't it?"

"Well, it was all you deserved."

"Listen, Doc. I used to play some professional ball. The thing I noticed was that when the team lost, they didn't fire the players."

Questions for Discussion

1. You are preaching to a church that is about to split over opinions on Christ's imminent return. Some members are angry with you. From Jesus' discourses, what principles can you apply as you prepare your message for next Sunday morning?
2. Why is a systematic outline so important in preparing a lecture?
3. How much did Jesus lecture to the crowds? How much to His disciples? In His teaching to the crowds, what did He plan to accomplish?
4. How much permanent impact can a lecture make?
5. How can you get a vocabulary that communicates? What can you do to choose the exact word? The piquant word?
6. A certain student is notorious for wasting time by asking trivial questions. He raises his hand again. Weigh your alternatives.
7. Humor has often worked to counter hostility, yet we can barely find a case in which Jesus used humor. How do you account for that? How does His example bear on our teaching?
8. Estimate the gains and losses in writing out a lecture in full. In what situations might it be worth the time?

Lecture Plan Checklist

1. How important is all this?
2. How urgently do I want my students to understand this?

I. ORGANIZATION

1. Is the content complete? Have I reached expertise on this subject?
2. Does the plan follow a distinct theme?
3. Do the main divisions fit together? Are the transitions clear?
4. Does this material need a handout? A visual?

II. PRESENTATION
   1. Can I teach this with authority? With zest?
   2. Am I confident enough of the material that I can handle questions on it?
   3. What is fresh about the way I am giving it?
   4. It is clear?

III. UNDERSTANDING
   1. Will this lecture enable them to explain the material to someone else?
   2. Does this suggest applications they may reach on their own?
   3. Will this provide students the wisdom to evaluate other information on this subject? Have I met God over this? Do I love these students?

Getting Interest

And the eyes of all them that were in the synagogue were fastened on him.

—Luke 4:20

And it came to pass, that, as the people pressed upon him to hear the word of God, he stood by the lake of Gennesaret.

—Luke 5:1

If we have the attention of our students, we can hope to teach them. If we do not have their attention, we might as well close up and leave.

How did Jesus do it? He was never boring. He fed five thousand and later four thousand. He worked miracles. Luke 6:17-19 says that the hope of being healed attracted throngs.

Did the miracles serve to get and hold attention? Doubtless, but the gospels hardly say so. When the Pharisees wanted to watch Him work a spectacular sign, He replied, "An evil and adulterous generation seeketh after a sign" (Matthew 12:39). How much spiritual impact did the miracles make? One indication may be that of the hundreds or thousands of people whom Jesus healed, the gospels name only a few. This suggests that when the gospels were being written one to three decades after the events, few of those He healed were still known to the Christian community in Israel.

Another view on the value of the miracles appears in John 6:26: "Verily, verily I say unto you, Ye seek me, not because ye saw the miracles, but because ye did eat of the loaves, and were filled."

The devil suggested to Jesus that He put on a spectacular by throwing Himself down from the pinnacle of the Temple. The Lord's refusal ought to warn us whenever we face the temptation to do something spectacular to hold our disciples' interest. If we want people to pay attention to our teaching, we do not need to fret because God withdrew miracles (compare 2 Timothy 4:20 with Acts 28:8-9); He gave us other ways to grip people.

WHAT ABOUT VISUALS?

The question of using visuals touches matters that are deep in our culture. What Scripture do we have for visual aids and attention-getting devices? Not much. The Old Testament ruled out just about every visual but the Tabernacle system itself. All the rest bordered on idolatry, and not until recent decades have the Jews shown much interest in the graphic arts. The prophets, notably Ezekiel, used a few devices, but like Christ, they relied chiefly on their message and their very presence to hold their hearers. Jesus' choice of visual aids makes a short list:

1. One or two little children (Matthew 18:1; Mark 9:36)
2. One basin of water (John 13)
3. One towel (John 13)
4. One fig tree (Matthew 21:19)

To try to expand this list we might add:

5. "This mountain" (Matthew 17:20)
6. Ravens (Luke 12:24)
7. Lilies (Luke 12:27)

If those last three look strained, they underscore the fact that Jesus did not rely on visuals to grip attention. Rather, He fascinated His hearers with His words and with His presence.

Jesus probably gave His final word on miracles when He told about the rich man in hell (Luke 16:27-31). The man did not want his five brothers to end up with him. He asked that Abraham send the beggar Lazarus to testify to them. Abraham replied that the ordinary testimony of Moses and the prophets offered the chance of eternal life.

"Nay, father Abraham: but if one went unto them from the dead, they will repent. And he said unto him, If they hear not Moses and the prophets, neither will they be persuaded though one rose from the dead" (16:30-31).

If the resurrection will not persuade the lost, it shows us something of the limitations of our overhead projectors. Our chalk, transparencies, and flannelgraph do help us teach, but we know that a teacher should not rely on those alone.

WHAT ABOUT HUMOR?

What about using humor to teach? We cannot doubt its powers to hold interest, disarm enemies, and encourage a warm and open spirit in a class. As products of a culture in which we love to have someone entertain us, we search the gospels for humor but find little. Did the writers lose it as they put the Aramaic into Greek? Unlikely. Are the jokes there, but we lack the cultural understanding to see them? Improbable.

If Jesus bore the fruit of the Spirit, we have to believe that He lived in joy. Writing of Calvary, Isaiah called Him the Man of Sorrows, but for the rest, Psalm 45:6-7 and Hebrews 1:9 say that God anointed Him with the oil of gladness above His fellows. We imagine His conviviality in Matthew 11:19: "The Son of man came eating and drinking," and in Luke 15:1, the friend of publicans and sinners. He used irony when He compared that generation to petulant children (Matthew 11:16-17). The only recorded laughter He provoked was in Jairus's house, but He was not being funny. Indeed, the word for ordinary laughter occurs only three times in the New Testament: Luke 6:21, 25, and James 4:9. The Bible is not a funny book, and Jesus is not a funny man. On the other hand, creation itself gives us the impression that the Creator does indeed have a sense of humor.

So where does that leave us? We still enjoy the incongruities of life, and we still find innocent things to joke about—but always with a certain restraint. We cannot find Scripture to justify our organized schools, so we regard them gratefully, tentatively, and humbly. In a similar way we enjoy our humor. We seek the joy of the Lord, and we thank Him for the chuckles along the way. We may use humor in our teaching, but we try to keep it from jamming out the message of the cross.

Now then, what can we learn from Jesus about how to hold the attention and interest of our hearers?

ASK FOR ATTENTION

"And He called the multitudes, and said unto them, Hear, and understand" (Matthew 15:10).

When we say, "Now listen to this," we can count on maybe fifteen seconds of attention. That might not seem like much, but it still helps our students. When we say, "Now get this," we are doing them the favor of helping them stay alert to teachings they need. True, we cannot use this often, or like a drug it may lose its effect. If we use it discreetly, it works. That means using it in a balanced combination with other ways of holding attention.

RAISE YOUR VOICE

"In the last day, that great day of the feast, Jesus stood and cried, saying, If any man thirst, let him come unto me and drink" (John 7:37).

If we shout something, we arrest attention. If we shout

everything, we lose attention. We numb our hearers, and we have nothing left to use for stress.

Incidentally, how loud was Jesus' voice? It must have been unusually loud and resonant. The day that He fed the five thousand He taught for much of the day, in the open air, to a crowd of many thousands. Matthew puts the number at five thousand men besides women and children.

In his autobiography, Benjamin Franklin recalled hearing George Whitefield preach on the streets of Philadelphia, and he marveled that the great evangelist was audible two blocks away. He then calculated that at a given moment thirty thousand persons could have heard Whitefield preach. On such an estimate we can believe that Jesus taught fifteen thousand, but we marvel that He was able to keep it up for hours on end.

APPEAL TO CURIOSITY

Jesus used the appeal to curiosity often and well. His encounter with the woman at the well is a study in itself, as He aroused curiosity in every one of His first five sentences: (1) He opened the conversation with an improbable request to a stranger. (2) He told her that if she knew who He was, she would have asked and received from Him living water. (3) When she asked how she could get it, He went on to say that His water would satisfy by springing up into everlasting life. (4) Then, saying, "Go call thy husband," He touched a sensitive nerve. (5) When she replied, "I have no husband," Jesus reviewed her past: five husbands, and now a man who was not her husband.

If He could get the curiosity of an individual, how did He arouse the curiosity of a crowd? Study John 6, and you find a whole series of examples. Try to estimate the impact of these:

Verse 29, "This is the work of God, that ye believe on him whom he hath sent." Then belief is a work?

Verse 32, "My Father giveth you the true bread from heaven." Your father? What bread?

Verse 33, "The bread of God is he which cometh down from heaven." How's that again? Then give us this bread.

Verse 35, "I am the bread of life."

Verse 37, "All that the Father giveth me shall come to me."

Verse 40, "And I will raise him up at the last day." Isn't this Jesus the carpenter, whose father and mother we know? What is this "I came down from heaven"?

Verse 44, "No man can come unto me, except the Father which hath sent me draw him."

Verse 48, "I am that bread of life."

Verse 51, "The bread which I shall give is my flesh." How shall this man give us his flesh to eat?

His listeners may not always have liked what they heard, but we can be sure that they didn't go to sleep.

How then do we arouse curiosity? It takes two steps. We begin with some sort of mystery; there is knowledge to be had. A man doing research is curious. Moses watched a flaming bush and became curious. A window display with a large, brass faucet, supported by nothing and connected to no pipe but gushing water into a wooden tub draws the curious.

We open with a statement such as:

> "Blessed are the poor in spirit."
>
> "Except ye eat the flesh of the Son of man and drink his blood, ye have no life in you."
>
> "In this sack I have a vial of medicine that has been fantastically successful in treating depression."
>
> "Not that which goeth into the mouth defileth a man, but that which cometh out of the mouth, this defileth a man."
>
> "You'll never believe what happened to me last Friday night."
>
> "Ye shall seek me, and shall not find me: and where I am, thither ye cannot come."

The second step in arousing curiosity is to promise the explanation but to suspend payment for a while. That builds suspense. Telling a story may do it. Numbers of Jesus' parables held the crowds' interest, and at the end Jesus made no attempt to explain what He meant by them.

The matter of curiosity leads to another general means of holding interest.

TELL A STORY

Illustrations have a whole clutch of values, and along with clarifying things, they hold people's interest. If we tell a story badly, it may confuse our students. If we have told it before, we may bore them. Otherwise stories are almost sure to work. Jesus used them often, especially with crowds. Young preachers rarely use them enough. C. S. Lewis used them brilliantly, and that may partially account for the continued large sale of his books.

Certain kinds of material hold attention, such as animal stories, funny stories, or stories about the uncanny; yet Jesus did not use them. We may suppose that He used parables primarily to instruct and incidentally to hold interest. But more of that in the next chapter.

INVOLVE YOUR HEARERS

As I mentioned in chapter 2, Jesus lectured well because He involved His hearers. If we want to do that, we talk to our students about themselves and about their interests. That means first talking directly to them, using the word *you*. We do that not only when we lecture but in all the teaching that we do. Jesus' teaching gives us some examples:

> Which of you shall have a friend, and shall go unto him at midnight, and say unto him, Friend, lend me three loaves. (Luke 11:5)

> Suppose ye that these Galileans were sinners above all the Galileans, because they suffered such things? I tell

you, Nay: but except ye repent, ye shall all likewise perish. Or those eighteen, upon whom the tower in Siloam
fell, and slew them, think ye that they were sinners above
all men that dwelt in Jerusalem? I tell you, Nay: but except ye repent, ye shall likewise perish. (Luke 13:3-5)

If the world hate you, ye know that it hated me before it
hated you. If ye were of the world, the world would love
his own: but because ye are not of the world, but I have
chosen you out of the world, therefore the world hateth
you. (John 15:18-19)

Got the idea? Get a tape of any acknowledged communicator, and count the second-person pronouns in any five
minutes of his speech. Rarely will the number fall below
thirty; it may run as high as sixty, or once every five seconds. Then notice whose interests he is talking about.
True, sometimes he may talk about himself and induce us
to identify with him. If you can do that, fine. But it is better
to talk to your hearers about themselves. They will listen to
you. Not only that; you do not put yourself in as much
danger of making your teaching an ego trip.

Ask Questions

"Which of you by taking thought can add one cubit
unto his stature?" (Matthew 6:27).

Asking questions can have all sorts of teaching values,
and one of them is to draw interest. Jesus' rhetorical questions provoked thought and helped to grip people. In
Matthew 5-7 (KJV), Jesus asks fifteen questions, and He
includes another six questions that His hearers might ask.
To what purpose? To get His hearers to think and to help
keep them interested. It is not hard; most of us do it automatically:

"Why are you here?"
"What do you want out of life?"
"Has anyone ever told you how you can have eternal
life?"

Ask something like any of those, and, for the moment at least, you have their attention.

CONFRONT

Conflict interests people, and conflict causes the fascination in competitive sports, in all drama, in court cases, and in war. We do not need to pick fights to attract crowds, although teachers before Abelard and preachers before Augustine have. Jesus did not pick fights, but He drew opposition. John 7 recorded His words to His brothers: "My time is not yet come: but your time is alway ready. The world cannot hate you; but me it hateth, because I testify of it, that the works thereof are evil. Go ye up unto this feast: I go not up yet unto this feast; for my time is not yet full come" (John 7:6-8).

Even in His absence He was the talk of Jerusalem.

We do not have to go out of our way to get into conflicts. When they come, it is time enough to accept them, because they bring an alert hearing for our position.

Our schools used to teach debating more than they do now; debates can be teaching devices. The conflict can draw interest and provide a hearing for our message.

Some conflicts face us constantly, and we gain attention by reminding our students of those. We are at war with the powers of darkness, and we fight those powers on our knees. We are in conflict with false doctrine. If our students have no great discernment as to those doctrines, Jesus' example authorizes us to clarify both.

He named parties even if He did not often name persons (compare Luke 12:1, 13:15, and 13:32). In recent history we have tended to go to extremes, either to shoot at anything that moves or else to warn our students of nothing, even the most flagrant heresies and syncretisms.

COMMUNICATE

The word *communicator* has become a jargon word, but it still has a value to us. It denotes a person who has an unusual ability to get his or her ideas across to others. The word connotes a number of qualities that we are accustomed to finding in such a person: warmth, fluency, confidence, and determination to make his ideas clear. His speech patterns and cadences are conversational rather than oratorical. Unlike many preachers, a communicator does not speak in holy tones; his words carry the tang of reality about them. Even from a lecture platform he talks as though he were sitting across the table from us. Sometimes he speaks formally but more often informally. We listen to him with delight.

To what extent did Jesus fit the description of a communicator? What do the gospels tell us about His eye contact? We cannot imagine Him as shifty-eyed or looking at the ground while He spoke. What do the gospels tell us about His manner? We cannot imagine that He taught in a stilted way, that He talked in a sing-song manner, or that He sounded like a train-caller. Indeed, can we imagine Him as anything else than a communicator? Everything in the gospels implies that He spoke directly, that He purposed that His disciples understand, and that He never spoke just to enjoy the rich sound of His own voice.

CONVEY MORAL EARNESTNESS

"The zeal of thine house hath eaten me up" (John 2:17). Jesus was never ethically neutral. As His enemies eyed Him in the synagogue, waiting to see if He would heal the withered hand on the Sabbath, He looked at them with anger, grieved at the hardness of their hearts (Mark 3:5).

Part of Jesus' ability to hold a crowd was His moral earnestness. There is something awesome about a competent teacher who is committed to a value system, especially a biblical system. He cannot be neutral. His commitment deepens the impact of everything he says.

Even in nonbiblical subjects earnestness attracts people. It applies to almost any subject. Driver education has life-and-death moral implications. Vocational education involves professional integrity and working well at a craft. Math demands integrity. Academics of any sort require disinterest, discipline, and precision. The professions once provided the moral leaders of the community, not just the financial leaders, and the studies of law and medicine are loaded with ethical implications. If moral earnestness applies in Bible classes, it is at home in almost any classroom, even if it rarely moralizes overtly.

John 7 records that the Pharisees sent officers to arrest Jesus (v. 32). Later the officers came back without Him. "Why have ye not brought him?" They replied, "Never man spake like this man" (John 7:45-46).

As we learn Scripture and reflect on it, as we confess and forsake known sins, as we seek victory over temptation, and as we discipline ourselves, we can hope that our very earnestness will help everything we do to get truth across to our students. Convictions mean principles we are willing to suffer for, and convictions carry weight as we teach.

Speak Wisdom

Expertise grips interest, but Jesus went beyond expertise. When a speaker has mastered a given field and shares that mastery, we usually follow with interest. We listen even if his delivery is mediocre. In Jesus we see more than mastery: "In whom are hid all the treasures of wisdom and knowledge" (Colossians 2:3). Only some of the treasures appear right away. Even the apostles sometimes seemed to take Him for granted. Yet they began to grasp that His knowledge was more than one level above theirs. They heard Him with fascination, because with everything else that He could show them, He spoke with spiritual wisdom.

Can we follow Him here? We can raise our voices, ask our students to listen, and find ways to pique their curiosity. We can tell stories, speak directly, and ask questions. We can impress and communicate. But wisdom? Isn't that reaching for the stars? Nearly so.

We can still make wisdom our life quest. We begin

with knowledge. Proverbs 1:7 says that the fear of the Lord is the beginning of knowledge. Proverbs 9:10 says that that fear is also the beginning of wisdom. Moses prayed that God would teach us to number our days that we might apply our hearts unto wisdom (Psalm 90:12), and in our good moments we pray that prayer. As we study we cultivate a wholesome fear of God, and as we meet Him in prayer we can hope that He will empower us to speak with wisdom.

Questions for Discussion

1. How interesting were Jesus' healings? What Scripture might give us reason to suppose that to His hearers the miracles became commonplace?
2. To what extent are attention and interest interchangeable words? How do they differ?
3. Why does an expert have an advantage in holding interest?
4. What effective uses of visual aids can you remember? How do you account for their success? What causes some visual aids to fail?
5. How does systematic lesson organization help to retain attention?
6. Why do some astounding statements grip attention and others fall flat?
7. Think about the proposition that a dull Bible class requires and therefore produces a higher level of spiritual life than a fascinating class does. Argue in favor of this proposition. Argue against it.

4

Illustrations

All these things spake Jesus unto the multitudes in parables; and without a parable spake he not unto them: that it might be fulfilled which was spoken by the prophet, saying, I will open my mouth in parables; I will utter things which have been kept secret from the foundation of the world.
—Matthew 13:34-35

Jesus was good at using illustrations, and we can learn from the way He used them. They are wonderfully useful to us.

The gospels give us some thirty-five parables, but our count depends on how we classify them. Do we include the houses on rock and sand (Matthew 7:24-27)? If so, do we count them as one parable or as two? We usually count the lost sheep, lost coin, and lost son as three, but the Lord seemed to count them all as parts of a single parable (Luke 15:3). Do we count the rich man and Lazarus as a parable? Many of us have blanched at calling it that for fear of seeming to deny the literal torments of hell. But we might as well count it for two reasons: (1) the Lord surely used it as an illustration; and (2) other illustrations He used are concrete examples of human experiences and not just comparisons (note the rich fool, the Good Samaritan, and the Pharisee and the publican).

Understanding Illustrations

Jesus' illustrations have several patterns, and one of them is that they all involve plausible human activity. Even with the seed and the barren fig tree, He mentions that a man—doubtless the same man—planted them. All the parables are plausible. Seven or eight include some improbable element, but in those the improbable element is the main point of the parable. The Good Samaritan acted improbably, but the point of it is that against all probability he helped the wounded man. The mustard plant is supposed to stay a shrub; the point of that parable is that it grew into a big tree. We wonder how a slave could pile up a debt approaching a billion dollars, but the point of the parable of the ten thousand talents is that he managed to do it. The good landowner paid all his day laborers the same full day's wage; no matter that some had worked only an hour. Improbable, but it is the sort of thing that an affluent planter just might do. The parables speak of human transactions taking place in real places. All the Lord's illustrations are plausible, and surely that includes the real torment of the lost.

Three of the parables mention God, and the prodigal confessed that he had sinned against heaven. Twenty-eight of the parables compare the Father or the Son to an authority figure: a king, landowner, builder, father, or sower. But whatever form the parables may take, they set out spiritual truth in terms that the human mind can visualize. We may explain them in abstractions, but the parables do not contain abstractions.

Getting Illustrations

How do we get illustrations? First by thinking hard about our material. As we concentrate our attention on the lesson plan in front of us, our mind will begin to bring up from its own depths analogies and examples that fit parts of our lesson plan. Some of those illustrations come from our past—our experiences and our study. Jesus' illustrations seem to come from His boundless knowledge of human activity; ours come from a limited knowledge of human activity. Still, our minds have a vast store to draw on, and we need only some demand or some suggestion to draw things out.

If experience will not give us quite the story we need, our mind will make up one for us. It still draws on the data already in it, but we put some of that data together to make a new story. For example, we want to clarify the injustice of refusing to forgive, but we can't remember an instance that gives us what we need. So we put several ideas together:

1. The offender is in debt.
2. Many debts have a cash equivalent.
3. Sometimes the creditor owes an even greater debt to someone else.
4. The human heart can be nasty, accepting forgiveness but then refusing to grant it to others.
5. Every professed believer owes an infinite debt to God.

Now let's make up a story out of those ideas. Suppose we begin with an employee who gets into debt with his foreman. Now let's say that the foreman is deep in debt to the wealthy landowner. How much do we owe God? An infinite amount? Let's say that the foreman got in impossibly deep—a billion dollars in debt. And let's set this in a country that still has indentured service and debtors' prisons. The landowner now calls the foreman to account and threatens a devastating foreclosure. The foreman pleads for time and makes desperate promises. The landowner is so moved at this display that he forgives the whole billion.

Now back to the original employee. How much do we have him owe the foreman? Three months of daily wages? Maybe three thousand dollars? Considerable, but trivial next to the billion from which the foreman was released. So the foreman comes to the employee and demands the three thousand. The employee pleads for time and promises to pay every bit of it. But no; the foreman gets the sheriff, forecloses, and strips the employee of everything that he has.

At that point we are ready to wrap up the story. It illustrates the awesome difference between the debt that we owed God, even in light of the considerable debts that other people may owe us. It illustrates the unfairness of holding another person to account when God has already forgiven us an infinity of guilt. It has the further value of making people see the unfairness in refusing to forgive. And we can set the whole story off with the words, "Now just suppose . . ."

We can induce our minds to come up with illustrations.

Now what did Jesus use His illustrations for? How can we use His examples as we illustrate our own teaching?

TELL STORIES

You want your class to listen? Then tell them stories.

To do that the way that Jesus did it may be harder than it seems. What He did effortlessly and, we suppose, at great length, may take us a great deal of preparation. While He held the crowds, He crafted His stories to convey spiritual truth. Each one has a story line, so that on the lowest level, it was easy to listen to; but at the same time it offered a spiritual truth that He did not explain to the crowd.

At the second level, by telling them stories, He was inviting them to think. The lecture system has a problem here. Often we cover material, explain it, and prove it. Then we expect that our students have eaten it almost without chewing. In return we expect them to regurgitate the material, using our own words so far as possible. Then we may marvel at how little they digest. Now many of us may have found ways to use a lecture to promote reflective thinking. In the parables Jesus seems to have used a good way to make people think.

One way to encourage reflective thinking is to do what Jesus did here: fascinate the large group with a story and then, when they are salivating for the explanation, to go into the next story without explaining the first one.

A third level of His intent was to attract the serious. When the crowd walked away, the disciples moved in close.

"And he said unto them, He that hath ears to hear, let him hear. And when he was alone, they that were about him with the twelve asked of him the parable" (Mark 4:9-10).

In the course of your lesson, you left something hanging. When you dismissed the class, a few of your students stayed to ask you about it. In that moment of rapport you had separated the disciples from the pupils, and the disciples got a learning experience that the others might have had.

Another purpose that Jesus had in using illustrations was to hold His people eternally accountable before the Father.

> And the disciples came, and said unto him, Why speakest thou unto them in parables? He answered and said unto them, Because it is given unto you to know the mysteries of the kingdom of heaven, but to them it is not given. For whosoever hath, to him shall be given, and he shall have more abundance: but whosoever hath not, from him shall be taken away even that he hath. Therefore speak I to them in parables: because they seeing see not; and hearing they hear not, neither do they understand. And in them is fulfilled the prophecy of Esaias, which saith, By hearing ye shall hear, and shall not understand; and seeing ye shall see, and shall not perceive: For this people's heart is waxed gross, and their ears are dull of hearing, and their eyes have they closed; lest at any time they should see with their eyes and hear with their ears, and should understand with their heart, and should be converted, and I should heal them. But blessed are your eyes, for they see: and your ears, for they hear. For verily I say unto you, That many prophets and righteous men have desired to see those things

which ye see, and have not seen them; and to hear those things which ye hear, and have not heard them. (Matthew 13:10-17)

Let us hope that we never have to teach those who have hardened their hearts against God while they pay their dues to their religious establishment. That group wants Bible teaching only so long as it does not include the spiritual truths that they need. God holds us to account as His servants to speak the truth; we represent Him and teach in His place. If people reject His words from our lips, even if those words come in parables, their blood is on their own heads, not on ours. In Jesus' case, Israel was accountable even for the enigmatical truth in His parables.

Introduce a Truth

How do we introduce a new idea in a course? One way is to point up to it, then to promise something new, and then to tell it. To introduce the aorist tense, or quadratic equations, or the reign of Henry VIII, that may work. But how do we introduce a spiritual truth that is new to our class? There may be a better way to do it than by beginning with an explanation. Setting it off with a narrative might do it better.

Suppose we want to present the coming era that will lead to the kingdom age. During that time Christ is going to lead a program of proclamation, which will get a mixed response, from instant rejection to glad acceptance. So we begin with a series of stories. In the first one, we tell about a farmer who goes out to sow a crop. He walks through his field, flinging out the seed to both sides. Some of it never sprouts. Some sprouts, but it dies right away. Some comes up among thorns; it grows but he gets no grain from it. The rest of the seed produces a crop, some a hundred for one, some sixty, and some thirty. Then we let our class think about that while we go on to our next story.

That will tease their minds, especially if we do not explain right away. It will not only challenge them to think, but it should generate maximum receptivity when we finally do explain.

Jesus told several of the parables to introduce spiritual concepts. Those that fit that analysis most easily are the seven parables in Matthew 13. To read a random dozen commentators could give us the idea that Jesus was trying to hide their meanings. On the other hand, commentators tend to agree closely if they agree first on a few principles:

1. The parables are consistent with one another and with biblical symbolism.
2. Non-symbolic elements are to be taken at face value.
3. The church is not Israel.

Other parables in this category would be the Good Samaritan, the pounds, the laborers in the vineyard, the ten virgins, the servants entrusted with the talents, and the extended account of the Good Shepherd in John 10. (This is the only real parable in John, and the writer labeled it with a different word for parable.) Parables that at least overlap this category are the importunate friend, the rich fool, and the lost sheep, coin, and son.

Do we want our students to understand something new, such as the indigenous principle in missions, or the basic ideas of existentialism, or the causes of the French revolution? A carefully-selected narrative makes a good opening, not just to gain interest but especially to introduce the problem.

CLARIFY A TRUTH

A third use of the illustration is to clarify a truth already given or known. For example, consider the situation mentioned above of the professing believer who has but a limited willingness to forgive another person. There is nothing wrong in telling him he shouldn't be like that, that he owes the Lord so much. However, by putting that in the form of a story, we speak to more than his thinking. We go straight to his feelings, and we may even get an emotional commitment from him. Now when we draw the link between him and our story, we not only make truth understandable; we make it vivid.

How can we expose the tentacles of covetousness? Jesus told the story of the rich fool, a story that any successful businessman could identify with, at least up to the tag line, "But God said unto him, Thou fool" (Luke 12:16-21).

How do we show the urgency of watching for Jesus' return? He told His disciples to be like men who wait for their lord to return from the wedding. How would we describe the glad welcome, the gala festivities? How would we relate the part where the Lord makes His servants recline to feast while He waits on them? Read Luke 12:35-40 to review how Jesus did it.

PLANT TRUTH IN HOSTILE MINDS

The gospels abound in examples of Jesus' use of parables to teach His enemies. How do we teach those who do not want to be taught? Within limits it can be done. We may question whether the enemies make any eternal gains through the truths that we inject into them. We are "as deceivers, yet true," but at least our stories make those people accountable, even though the bystanders get the spiritual benefits.

A quibbler traps himself into admitting that love's duty transcends all his legalisms. You gently confirm his admission. Now how can he squirm out of it? He asks who the neighbor is that he is supposed to love as himself. If you tell him that his neighbor is the next stranger to come along, you can predict his next quibble. But you begin a story and get his interest; you build the details of the man who fell among bandits, and of the stranger who despite the danger and bother came to his aid. Then you ask, "Which was neighbor to the man who fell among the bandits?" What can he say?

Jesus used the same means to warn the elders who were plotting to murder Him. He gave them three parables (Matthew 21:28—22:14). The first parable, that of the two sons, exposed their disobedience. The second parable, the story of the wicked husbandmen, ripped the mask from their hatred, exposed their rotten system, and warned them of the Father's impending wrath. The third parable, the marriage feast, again showed their rebellion and predicted that God would replace the lot of them.

Of the other examples of using parables to teach the hostile, we may include the two debtors (Luke 7:41-42), the barren fig tree (Luke 13:6-9), the great supper (Luke 14:16-24), the lost sheep, coin, and son, the rich man and Lazarus, and even Luke's account of the mustard seed and the leaven (13:18-21).

All of those show the power of narrative to get a hearing. They all show the power to plant an idea in a hostile mind. As advertisers know, there is such a thing as the indirect approach; a hint of an idea may pay off long afterward. In confronting an alert or hostile mind, that may be the only approach available. However, of the seeds that Jesus planted that way, we may wonder what positive fruit He ever received. One hint of an answer comes in Acts 6:7, "And the word of God increased; and the number of the disciples multiplied in Jerusalem greatly; and a great company of the priests were obedient to the faith." Why the priests? Partly because of the testimony of the disciples. But why the priests as opposed to any other select group? Partly because they knew most about the rending of the Temple veil. But at least some of those conversions may trace to the delayed effect of the parables that they had resisted but still listened to.

How do we minister to those who do not want our message? By our consistent bearing of the Spirit's fruit. Beyond that, if we can present narratives that contain spiritual truth, we can plant mental time bombs that do more than make sinners accountable before the eternal justice. We may plant ideas that the Holy Spirit can use some day.

Questions for Discussion

1. Why do the parables include no miracles, magical elements, or talking trees?
2. Weigh the arguments for and against calling Luke 16:19-31 a parable.
3. What suggestions can you offer to the teacher who insists that he simply cannot come up with illustrations for his lesson plans?
4. Almost any narrative will draw attention. How can you find the kind of story that will introduce an idea?
5. Are not stories useful in winning over hostile or skeptical students? Then how much did Jesus' parables accomplish in winning over the skeptical? To what extent do our skeptics resemble His?
6. What connection is there between being a communicator and having the ability to illustrate with the right narrative?

5

Obscurities, Enigmas, and Paradoxes

The Jews therefore strove among themselves, saying, How can this man give us his flesh to eat?
—John 6:52

Then said the Jews among themselves, Whither will he go, that we shall not find him? What manner of saying is this that he said, Ye shall seek me, and shall not find me: and where I am, thither ye cannot come?
—John 7:35-36

"No teaching is complete that does not issue in plain and intelligent expression of the lesson; this means that the expression should be in the language of the child, and not mere repetition of ready-made definitions of someone else, in words very likely in many cases to be totally unfamiliar" (Gregory, *The Seven Laws of Teaching*, p. 47).

Does anything seem more self-evident than that a teacher ought to be clear? How can we get anything across if we do not state it in the plainest terms that we have? Yet Jesus seemed to flout that rule all through His ministry, and we rightly call Him the master Teacher. He deliberately said things that His hearers did not understand. We have some things to learn from Him.

The first New Testament discourse, the Sermon on the Mount, opens with nine statements, each beginning with the word *blessed*. Those statements form one of the most familiar passages in the Bible, the Beatitudes. However, to the human mind, every one of them is absurd and repugnant to common sense. Any paperback on how to climb the corporate ladder could fittingly list the opposites of those in its first chapter. To the natural mind, the Beatitudes do not make sense.

Go on through the Sermon on the Mount, and you find more. It is a staggering demand that our righteousness must exceed that of the scribes and the Pharisees. More such demands follow, touching anger and lust. Then Jesus talks about plucking out an eye or cutting off a hand —understandable hyperbole. But in the rest of the chapter He makes five more demands, each so great that we want Him to slow down and explain.

John's gospel is barely into Jesus' ministry when it records His answer to the Jews: "Destroy this temple, and in three days I will raise it up" (John 2:19). They never figured out that one. In chapter 3 Jesus tells Nicodemus to be born again, and although that expression is commonplace to us, it baffled him. Indeed, verse 5 has baffled Christians ever since John recorded it: "Verily, verily, I say unto thee, Except a man be born of water and of the Spirit, he cannot enter into the kingdom of God."

Lord, why did You do that to us?

We can explain some of Jesus' obscurities as figures of speech. We can explain others as obscure only because we are earth-bound listeners to One who knows heaven and speaks its language. Why wouldn't many of His statements seem odd, just as the casual conversation of any English-speaking foreigner shines with strange experiences, insights, and customs?

Indeed, what makes a statement obscure?

1. Some statements defy common sense, as do the Beatitudes.

2. Some statements defy a traditional understanding of the Bible, such as Jesus' statements on divorce.
3. Some statements have the appearance of being self-contradictory, such as, "Many that are first shall be last: and the last shall be first."
4. Some put our reasoning to the test, as His word on the convicting work of the Holy Spirit: "Of righteousness, because I go to my Father, and ye see me no more."

Many of Jesus' obscurities were deliberate teaching devices, and from those we have things to learn. We can be sure that He was never obscure for obscurity's sake, or that He wanted to impress, or that He wanted to appear deep. He used obscurities in order to teach, and that should be our only motivation as well.

INDUCE PEOPLE TO THINK

Much of teaching seems designed to tell people what to think. It is harder to teach them how to think.

A friend recently spoke at a teachers' meeting on the theory of teaching and pressed the idea that at any level the students should be able to think through the material, test its validity, explain it back, and apply it in related situations. Short of those payoffs, we simply cannot consider it teaching. Another teacher argued against that, saying it was expecting too much, especially at the lower levels. But the discussion leader was at that time teaching in an elementary school and meeting those objectives at the lower levels.

How do we induce our students to think? Indeed, how much does our teaching help or hinder them from finding truth for themselves? We would probably all agree that they gain most from what they learn for themselves. If we somehow led, pointed, or drove them to learn, so much satisfaction for us. However, they have to do the learning, and our teaching is to help them to do this.

How did Jesus do it? Go over your own memories of such statements as these:

> And from the days of John the Baptist until now the kingdom suffereth violence, and the violent take it by force. (Matthew 11:12)

> O ye of little faith, why reason ye among yourselves, because ye have brought no bread? Do ye not yet understand, neither remember the five loaves of the five thousand, and how many baskets ye took up? Neither the seven loaves of the four thousand, and how many baskets ye took up? How is it that ye do not understand that I spake it not to you concerning bread, that ye should beware the leaven of the Pharisees and of the Sadducees? (Matthew 16:8-11)

> Where, Lord? And he said unto them, Wheresoever the body is, thither will the eagles be gathered together. (Luke 17:37)

Is there one of us who has not stared at such statements as those—and done some thinking? Even if on one or two we have not yet come to our final conclusions, we have pondered, looked up words, read some commentaries, and learned something for ourselves. Now how do we induce our students to do that? It might not be easy.

Where do we start? Perhaps where two of these three examples occur, at the end of the lesson. We plan the closing remark that will set off thinking after class, a remark that may even spark conversation:

"Just remember, you're not saved by asking Jesus to come into your heart."

"Just remember, Jesus was not a Christian."

"If you teach people to tithe, you will deprive them of all sorts of spiritual blessings."

And then, of course, we dismiss the class without explaining.

A caution has to go with this method. We had better be prepared to follow up on any of these the next class period. Challenging thought is like giving an allowance; we don't know what the recipient is going to spend it on, but we have to take the chance if he is ever to learn intelligent choices. Challenging the students to think means risking that they may make wrong choices. Drawing them out in conversation should give an idea how the risk paid off and whether we will need to challenge wrong reasoning.

A second caution is that we must not plant doubts about Scripture or harden a conscience. Liberal teachers have been doing those things for years, to draw young people away from the faith once delivered. Such teachers flatter themselves that they are teaching students to think, when in reality they are only teaching them something to think. They replace one set of values with another, swapping humanistic values for conservative ones.

STARTLE THE SMUG

A man I know was trying to witness to a convict. To every statement or Bible verse, the inmate answered, "Yes, that's right. Yes, yes, that's right." In desperation my friend asked, "Man, do you realize that you're on your way to hell?"

"That's right—huh?"

Nice double take. How do you get through to people who think that everything is all right, when everything is *not* all right?

Late in Jesus' ministry the apostles were exuding a certain confidence. They had worked miracles and preached; they had absorbed three years of His teaching, and they had attained a certain familiarity with Him that others could only envy. In that frame of mind they asked Jesus who is the greatest in the kingdom of heaven. His answer must have been the surprise of the year. He took a little child (the Greek testament carefully avoids the gender) and stood it in the open. Then He said, "Verily I say unto you, Except ye be converted, and become as little children, ye shall not enter into the kingdom of heaven. Whosoever therefore shall humble himself as this little child, the same is greatest in the kingdom of heaven" (Matthew 18:3-4).

That seemed to close the subject for a while. It baffled them.

In the next chapter He did it again. First He demolished the Pharisees for their easy view of divorce. Thereupon the disciples tried out the idea that it is good not to marry at all. If we wonder what was in their minds, we may also wonder what they understood of Jesus' reply: "For there are some eunuchs, which were so born from their mother's womb: and there are some eunuchs, which were made eunuchs of men: and there be eunuchs, which have made themselves eunuchs for the kingdon of heaven's sake. He that is able to receive it, let him receive it" (Matthew 19:12).

Later in the same chapter He baffled them again, as the rich young ruler was walking away: "Verily I say unto you, That a rich man shall hardly enter into the kingdom of heaven" (19:23). That ended their confidence that they understood the book of Deuteronomy, especially chapter 28 (see Matthew 19:24-25).

Then Peter remarked that they had forsaken everything to follow Him; what were they going to get for it? Jesus gave him two answers: (1) that one day they would sit on twelve thrones judging the tribes of Israel, but (2) "many that are first shall be last, and the last shall be first." That puzzle led to the parable, beginning in chapter 20, of the laborers in the vineyard. This parable itself has puzzled many.

The last obscurity in this series came when James, John, and their mother asked for the choice seats in the kingdom. The others took that as effrontery, possibly wondering why they had not asked first. Then Jesus summarized the matter. "But whosoever will be great among you, let him be your servant; and whosoever will be chief among you, let him be your slave: even as the Son of man came not to be served, but to serve, and to give his life a ransom for many" (Matthew 20:26-28; author's trans.).

By now they must have begun to catch on: the path along which Jesus leads us is no ego trip.

We have all seen the wreckage of disciples whom someone pushed too far too fast. A young person who passes driver's training shouldn't think that as a result he understands carburetion. Can we caution our disciples after their first few platform successes? God's device in extreme cases is to let them fail. Jesus at least went to great lengths to head off Peter from the three denials. How can we try to do it? One way might be through the enigmatic remark.

EXPRESS HEAVEN'S TRUTH

How remote is heaven from earth? Could we measure the distance in light years? To the redeemed, heaven is near, only a gasp and a heartbeat away. To the natural mind, heaven is a cartoon world of clouds, robes, harps, and fatuous people with cardboard haloes. To many believers heaven is a nebulous realm that they would rather not go to just yet. So how do we translate heaven to them while we wait for God to translate us to heaven?

We do not have to try to find enigmatic ways to tell divine truth. Jesus told Nicodemus that a person has to be born from above, or born again, to see the kingdom. Once we grasp that truth the need for rebirth seems elementary; to Nicodemus it made no sense. Jesus told the Jews, "If a man keep my saying, he shall never see death" (John 8:51). We can accept that statement as psychologically true. Whatever an unbeliever goes through at death, or whatever we imagine him to go through, the believer passes directly from consciousness or coma to another consciousness. If that is not what those at the deathbed see, no matter. Heaven's truth is bound to be enigmatic.

REBUKE THE SCOFFER

If someone hates God, and we answer his questions with an obscurity, have we used a teaching device? Perhaps not, but in an encounter it is a legitimate way to rebuke such a mind. Jesus did it often.

To the mourners in Jairus's house He said that the girl was only sleeping. "They laughed him to scorn" (Luke 8: 53).

To Pharisees and Sadducees who wanted a sign from heaven, He said that the only sign that they would get was the sign of the prophet Jonah (Matthew 16:4).

Someone asked if only a few would be saved. Jesus told him to strive to enter in at the narrow gate (Luke 13:24).

Pharisees warned Him of Herod. Jesus said, "Go ye, and tell that fox, Behold, I cast out devils, and I do cures today and to morrow, and the third day I shall be perfected" (Luke 13:32).

They demanded to know when the kingdom should come. He answered, "The kingdom of God cometh not with observation: Neither shall they say, Lo here! or, lo there! for, behold, the kingdom of God is within you" (Luke 17:20-21).

They accused Him of speaking of God as His Father. He quoted the psalm that said, "I have said, Ye are gods" (Psalm 82:6). Whether they understood, they surely remembered the next lines, which say, "And all of you are children of the most High. But ye shall die like men, and fall like one of the princes."

How then do we apply this? Solomon implied that there is no good way to answer a fool according to his folly (Proverbs 26:4-5). If there is such a way, it must be in the way that Jesus did it. He did not often give straight teaching to His enemies; He often gave them riddles. If we can think fast enough in corresponding situations, we might offer riddles.

Most of us do not think fast enough to pull that off. It still is a scriptural device for countering the questions of those who do not want our instruction anyway.

PLANT TIME-DELAY CHARGES

Jesus showed at least one other use for the statement that His disciples did not understand. It was His practice to make statements that would seem obscure but would make sense later on. Almost all of His predictions of the cross and of the resurrection fall into this class. The disciples heard him without hearing. They had no way to fit Calvary into their doctrine of the messianic reign. John 12:12-16 says that they understood later.

We have many things to teach that our students are not ready for, things that we must somehow get into their minds. The world is bombarding our children with erotic stimuli barely dreamed of a generation ago, and few of our children seem equipped to cope with them. How much less are they ready to understand the biblical harmony in love, marriage, and sex—and in that order? We shall have to impart values all along the way, but some of those values they will understand only later and after they have graduated from our discipling. How do we teach an older child that in the moment of passion all the values and divine commands still apply? We will need to attach time-delay fuses to our admonitions, so that what they barely understand now they will remember when the need arises.

Some of our young people have barely reached the maturity to keep up payments and insurance on a motorcycle, and we are trying to train them for Christian service. We try to teach them to exegete the Bible, comfort the bereaved, and moderate a business meeting. What hope can we have that five years hence they will consult any notes we have dictated? Again, we have to form some particularly memorable statements that can come back at the moment of need.

We long to produce faithful missionaries. If they purpose in Bible school to serve abroad, years of preparation are waiting for them. After they graduate, they may take more years in graduate school. Some may work for years to pay off student loans. Beyond that there may be years of deputation and then a year or more in language study. How can we teach them what they will need five to ten years hence? They can learn language and truck repair on the field. What they will need from us they will have to remember. How memorable can we make our teaching? Some sentences will be more memorable than most paragraphs, and those sentences will seem mysterious. It may well sound like one of these:

If you have the right view of God's sovereignty, it will help your soul-winning.

If you haven't the time to pray, prayer will be your best time-saver.

If you think that foreign service will make you holy, forget it. You have to take your holiness with you, and the foreign field will do all it can to take your holiness away from you.

Something may stick.

To answer the scorners takes a fast mind. To frame the remark that will come back years later must take at least as much Holy Spirit wisdom.

Questions for Discussion

1. How much do we need to work at puzzling our students? How often or how rarely do we need to use that kind of statement?
2. What examples can you remember of obscurities that forced you to think? What teachers were good at them?
3. What Bible passages have by their obscurity made you think? How would you explain to someone else the way the process worked?
4. What can we do to make a remark memorable?
5. How can we cut a swollen ego down to size without crushing a person's spirit and losing him altogether?
6. When a teacher baffles a student, what do you see that may endanger the teacher himself?

Asking Questions

Whom do men say that I the Son of man am?
— Matthew 16:13

But whom say ye that I am?
— Matthew 16:15

If our first-line teaching device has been the lecture, probably our second device is the question. It has all sorts of uses, and it works in almost any situation. Even in the middle of a lecture to a throng, even when it expects no one to give an answer, it is still a useful rhetorical device. We can question a crowd or an individual; we can question friends or enemies.

The supreme value of almost any question is that it invites a person to think. Doubtless some sort of activity goes on in every mind all the time, awake or asleep. How much of it does the person any good or concerns him about eternal things is another matter. Yet we might agree that thinking on eternal things is just about all that matters, and here Jesus' concern is our concern. How do we induce people to think about God and about what matters to Him? Partly by asking them the sort of question that will invite them to think.

Another value of asking questions is that almost any mind can play. To produce a brilliant obscurity, a statement that says exactly what the situation needs, takes a fast mind. Yet to ask the question that serves the teaching purpose is something that just about any one of us can do.

A Russian Communist was lecturing on the wonders of atheism. Finally a peasant woman got the chance to ask a question: "I received Christ years ago, and He has given me peace in my heart and the hope of heaven when I die. If your teaching is right, what have I lost?"

"Not very much," he said.

"If I am right and you are wrong, what will you lose?"

"I prefer not to answer that question."

Arnold Schultz once took a class through the Oriental Institute in Chicago. As Dr. Schultz later described the occasion, the guide was showing the group an Egyptian image of a cow. He explained that the cow was an exact replica of the golden calf that Aaron made at Sinai. One of the students asked, "How do you know?"

Some seconds later the guide answered, "Let's move on to the next exhibit."

Jesus' questions sprang from wisdom itself, but His method is open to all of us. It takes no great mind to frame the questions that teach, that encourage thought, and that draw out a class. Who can't get an answer from a student and then ask, "What else?" One guideline might be not to ask questions that invite yes or no for their answers; but once in a while even Jesus asked such questions.

So how did Jesus use questions in His teaching? The gospels give us several ways.

OPEN A CONVERSATION

A question is a natural way to begin a conversation:

> Then Jesus turned, and saw them following, and saith unto them, What seek ye? (John 1:38)

> Wilt thou be made whole? (John 5:6)

> Woman, where are thine accusers? (John 8:10)

What manner of communications are these that ye have one to another, as ye walk, and are sad? (Luke 24:17)

Children, have ye any meat? (John 21:5)

Find what works for you; it isn't hard.

PRERARE FOR INSTRUCTION

"What thinkest thou, Simon? of whom do the kings of the earth take custom or tribute? of their own children, or of strangers? (Matthew 17:25).

That question provides an example that we can use. The Lord asked it in order to introduce an analogy. Might we want to persuade a class that a lecture needs an outline? We might begin with, "Now think for a moment. What would happen to your posture if your spinal column were to crumble, neck to pelvis?"

"Dost thou believe on the Son of God?" (John 9:35).

In this case the Lord used a question to state a doctrine. While the question seems to have invited a yes or no answer, it carried a load of meaning. The man once blind had come to some insight; he knew that Jesus was a man of God. The Lord's question dropped on him like a rock: godliness is one thing; deity is a vastly higher matter. The simple question introduced it. Earnest Jew that the man was, he understood the awesome claim and accepted it.

How do we do it? By opening with just such questions as:

"Do you believe that God will actually raise human bodies from the dead?"

"Have you ever thought about what it must be like to be in hell?"

"How can a just God let guilty men off? Have you ever thought about that?"

Jesus and the crowd were approaching the tomb of Lazarus. Jesus said to whoever was listening, "Take away the stone." Martha protested. Jesus said to her, "I told you, didn't I, that if you would believe, you will see the glory of God?" (John 11:40; author's trans.). Suppose He had put it in the form of a statement. Even in that charged setting, would it have had the same effect?

INDUCE REFLECTION

Probably every teacher can remember the times when his best insights came to him after he thought he had finished his lesson plan, not during the process. The work of preparation paid off in getting his mind to reflect, and the reflection paid off in deepened understanding and originality.

Now if reflection enriches us, it is bound to enrich our students. How can we convey to them this wealth? It is not a commodity or a bag of coins that we can hand to them. It is more like a thirst that we can cause by salting their tongues. So how did Jesus do it?

James and John came wanting to sit at His side in His kingdom. It was their mother who made the actual request. Jesus answered them, "You do not understand what you are asking (even though you rightly acknowledge My supremacy). Are you able to sip the cup that I am about to drink to the bottom? Or the plunge that I am undergoing, are you able to accept it at all?" (Matthew 20:22; author's trans.). They seemed to answer so easily, "We are able." But we may suppose that they never forgot the question.

Jesus was washing the feet of the disciples. As we might expect, He had trouble when He got to Peter. Eventually He finished His task and replaced His garments. Then He asked, "Know ye what I have done unto you?" The word for "know" implies a learning process; "have done" says that He did it finally. It was an act with profound implications for doctrine and for service. We may wonder if we yet have more than a fingernail hold on what He was teaching. But the question that followed the act invited them to reflect.

So how do *we* do it?

Possibly our best means of getting students to reflect is to spend time of our own in reflection. The example can be contagious; imaginative teachers and preachers seem to catch their torch from older teachers and preachers they admire. Your own experience should bear this out, and it underscores our obligation to be worthy models for our students to pattern their thought lives after.

On the basis of our example we can assign projects that demand reflection. Then we can commend all evidences of reflective thinking and reward it. We can do that for all those with whom we are in regular and structured contact, meaning in classes or in discipleship arrangements. But what about our informal teaching as well, and what about situations in which we are not able to make assignments?

In all our teaching we frame questions that will challenge thought. Many of those questions will begin with the word *why*.

"Why does God delay to punish sin? And why else?"

"How do we decide which prayers to pray with confidence and which to pray with the words 'if it be Thy will'?"

"Why did Jesus choose Judas to be an apostle?"

In passing, we might ask ourselves why Jesus did not use questions in situations that we take for granted. If discussions and buzz groups promote reflection, why have we no record that Jesus ever led one or overtly structured one? In fact the disciples did discuss things informally (Mark 9:34), and Jesus doubtless did instigate at least one such discussion (Matthew 16:6-7). But we may well wonder why He did not actually set up discussions. The answer to this problem may lie in Jesus' view of truth, that truth is absolute and that a consensus may be a misleading approach to the absolute.

A second such matter that we might ponder is Jesus' omission, even His refusal, to use the Socratic method. Not once do the gospels record a long series of questions and answers with His disciples. Such a series would lead them step-by-step to conclusions that their teacher had already set. Along the way His line of questions would expose their fallacies and inconsistencies. It appears that Jesus borrowed nothing from Socrates.

When such an approach would seem so natural in His encounters with His disciples, we might well reflect on that. We might exclude any cultural reasons, which would turn on a Jewish aversion to Greek modes of thought. Jesus' reasons probably went deeper. The Socratic method takes for granted the authority of human reason and worships at its shrine. None of his pupils was as brilliant as Socrates; but his method tantalized their minds with the hope that in time they too could discover truth and wisdom.

Jesus did not lead His disciples to discover truth; He revealed truth to them. A grand canyon separates revelation from reason, Christ from Socrates. Socrates' method supposes that truth is in your mind already; you just need Socrates to draw it out. Jesus' revelations are not already in your mind, even though He expressed surprise when men failed to grasp Old Testament truth. "You are the teacher of Israel, and you do not understand these things?" (John 3:10; author's trans.).

Another difference here is that Socrates gave his pupils only a limited hope of attaining their teacher's wisdom. Jesus, on the other hand, gave His disciples about as much truth as they could handle, and then He promised them His Spirit. Through the Holy Spirit the New Testament writers could carry on the ministry of revelation—but not by drawing out their Timothies and Tituses with chains of brilliant questions.

PULL HEARERS UP SHORT

There comes a time in the teaching process when our disciples are plainly on a wrong track. They are toying with a wrong doctrine, or they are getting cocky, or they are trying to go in their own strength. In cases such as those, Jesus used questions to pull His disciples up short.

The apostles were facing a terrible storm. As Jesus lay asleep in the stern—the only time the gospels record that He slept—waves were washing into the boat. The men held off as long as they dared. Finally in panic they woke Him and demanded, "Doesn't it matter to You that we are perishing?"

Jesus then calmed the storm. In the sudden stillness that followed, He asked, "Why are ye so fearful? how is it that ye have no faith?" (Mark 4:35-41). Mark went on to say that they feared exceedingly. Why not? How much longer would He have waited?

Some months later Peter tried walking on water. He was doing all right until he looked around. Jesus rescued Peter and asked almost the same question: "O thou of little faith, wherefore didst thou doubt?" (Matthew 14:31). Further examples of pulling people up short might include Matthew 16:8; Luke 12:26; 24:38; John 3:10-12; 4:35; 10:32; 11:26; 13:38; 16:31; 21:15-17; and especially 21:22.

How do we do it? At the very least, let us try to do it gently. We may well wonder how many disciples we have lost to Christian service by losing our patience with them. I remember reading years ago about an animal trainer who was asked to explain his unusual success. He replied, "I never humiliate an animal."

In those times when we need to pull a student up short, may our words show as much wisdom.

PROBE FOR MOTIVES

In some circles it is considered bad form to question motive. For teachers the problem is not that simple. True, love does not impute evil motives (1 Corinthians 13:5, 7). The Bible discerns motives (Hebrews 4:12), and Jesus questioned motives, those of His enemies (Matthew 22:18) and those of His disciples (Matthew 26:10). As teachers we need to concern ourselves about our people's motives: what good is a man's honesty if it stems from a clumsiness at picking locks? What virtue is in the husband who is faithful to his wife because he hasn't enough money to carry on an affair?

Recent books on counseling have stressed that we ask "what?" not "why?" To ask why seems to play into the hands of the Freudians and to invite the counselee to blame others for his failures. However, Jesus often asked why, and we can find in Him precious little comfort for the impulse to blame our sins on society.

If we would help our students to cleanse their motives, we can well ask such questions as, "Why do you say that?" If we word it, "What makes you say that?" we may be inviting the wrong sort of answer. Hence our questions:

"Why do you feel that way?"
"Why do you want to succeed at this?"
"Why do you want to learn Greek?"
"Search your heart. Was that the real reason?"

Are those questions too personal to put to someone? As long as we ask in love, as long as our own motives are pure, and as long as we can keep confidences, we have a certain liberty to ask. Jesus' questions to Peter could hardly get more personal. "Simon, son of Jonas, lovest thou me more than these?"

It may be true that God waits to judge motives, and we are on slippery ground to judge the motives of others. Most assuredly, however, each believer, each disciple, must search his own motives. If he finds that his wonderful works spring from corrupt or selfish motives, either he will judge and condemn his motives, or else he will open himself to a dangerous series of evils that God will judge. A little leaven will go on corrupting the whole lump. Our disciples need to understand that, and we fail in our duty to them if we neglect to caution them about their motives.

FORCE AN ADMISSION

"Which of you convinceth me of sin? And if I say the truth, why do ye not believe me?" (John 8:46).

"Which now of these three, thinkest thou, was neighbour unto him that fell among the thieves?" (Luke 10:36).

An obvious pedagogic use of the question comes in the confrontation. Some of our students may be virtual hecklers. On the other hand, some of our earnest disciples will pick up ideas that, however unscriptural, are still hard to dislodge. In such cases we might lecture, but our stubborn hearer will just tighten the strap on his protective helmet. Is there any way to pry open his mind? Lacking that, is there any way to curb his opposition? One good approach is the right question:

"I can see how you might feel that way, but have you got even one Bible verse for it?"

"All right, how much clock time have you spent praying about this?"

"If Jesus had been in your position, what would He have done?"

ANSWER A QUESTION

"By what authority doest thou these things? and who gave thee this authority? And Jesus answered and said unto them, I also will ask you one thing" (Matthew 21:23-24).

"Why is it that every time I ask you something, you answer it with a question?"

"Well, why not?"

Some questions invite that sort of answer, especially when we do not want to let someone drive us against the wall. When he asks in sarcasm or malice, or when he asks in the evident hope of venting some cherished opinion, how do we parry the thrust? The right question just might be our means. He demands, "Are you implying that you believe in election?"

"Well, let me ask you one. Do you pray for the salvation of the lost?"

Or someone asks for your explanation of a certain verse. You tell him what the verse means. He then asks, "Do you realize that none of the nineteen commentaries in our library takes the view that you just gave?"

"Well, if you have already accepted their opinions, why did you ask me for mine?"

A soft answer turneth away wrath, and there may be a soft enough way to answer his question.

A second reason for answering with a question is that it buys a little time to reflect on the matter. If we simply do not know the answer, we might as well admit it frankly. The same goes for the question we are embarrassed to answer. To give an honest refusal is one thing. To try to bluff our way is either dishonest or dangerous. To counter with a question gains us some time to remember what we need, or else to frame the best answer that we can. Two common responses to the difficult question are: "That's a good question" and "I'm glad that you asked that question." But both responses have come to convey the reverse of what they affirm. We might do better to ask, "Why do you ask that question?" or, "What do you have in mind?"

A third reason to answer with a question is to keep the reflection going. As teachers we delight to instruct, to explain, and to inform. If instruction is what the student is asking and perhaps even paying for, should we not hand it to him? Not always. We all sense those times when we need to instruct and those times when we injure by too quickly instructing. We would do more good by prolonging the thought process. In these latter cases, we might do better to answer questions by asking questions. Thereby we do more than merely inform—we educate.

Questions for Discussion

1. What examples can you remember of questions that drove you to think?
2. Why didn't Jesus organize formal discussion groups?
3. Why did Jesus not use the Socratic method of teaching?
4. Since discussion groups seem to be so useful to a teacher, what biblical justification do we have for using them? How do we make them work? What limitations do they have?
5. What importance do you see in searching our own motives? in searching our students' motives? What biblical basis do we have to question their motives?
6. How can we cultivate the ability to ask the right question in a confrontation?

7

Short Bits
of
Instruction

*Then Jesus sent the multitude away, and went into
the house: and his disciples came unto him, saying,
Declare unto us the parable of the tares of the field.*
—Matthew 13:36

How many parallel ministries have you carried on at a
time? A pastor may carry on parallel ministries,
preaching to his members on Sundays, discipling a few
leaders, and perhaps teaching a Thursday noon Bible
study at some corporation headquarters. A missionary
might carry on a number of ministries in a given term,
preaching in a church, teaching in a Bible school, discipling one or more national workers, witnessing to individuals, writing. So Jesus carried on parallel ministries with
crowds and at the same time with His disciples. As the gospels record it, the crowds usually got extended discourses,
whereas the disciples got only a few such discourses. Much
of the ministry to them came in short bursts of instruction,
but instruction that the disciples found memorable.

Another matter here seems even more important: Jesus' ministry to the disciples took place wholly in informal
settings. We read of no classrooms, no structured meet-
ings, no regular lesson plans or agendas. How does that
touch us? We need to do what so many have done; we need
to give serious thought to the effect of formal situations on
learning. On the one hand, Jesus did not avoid teaching in

structured situations; eight distinct times the gospels record that He taught in synagogues, and Mark 1:39 says
that He preached in them. On the other hand, He taught a
great deal outside the structured situations, and His example is one that some of us have barely followed.

How do we cut through the formality and make use of
the informal setting? Primarily through two means. The
first is the way we use the classrooms we have. If we set
them up in the traditional manner, chairs lined up facing
the front, we may be able to get some truths and values
across. Some of us may stand and dictate notes into the students' notebooks. But if we think that much learning takes
place, we may find out that we have been flattering ourselves. By varying our approach, manner, methods, and visuals, we can hope to transcend the structured situation
and induce more learning. If we use all possible means to
grip attention and stimulate curiosity, we can hope to induce still more learning. But the beginning of that may
well require rearranging the classroom, trying to find any
means to break the mold and alter the pattern.

A second way to break the formality is to get out of the
classroom altogether. The tour is one way to get out; visit a
museum, a gallery, or a factory. Or find a way to take the
group outdoors. Sound like too much trouble? Are you
concerned about having to do without chalkboard, overhead, and podium? About competing with the glare and
traffic? About trying to project your voice in the open air?
Or about what the grass might do to your light suit if you
sat down to teach? Or are you interested in the change of
pace that such an opportunity would give? Jesus often
taught outside.

With a small group, why not recess to a local restau-
rant? With coffee or hot chocolate on the table, the class
may come alive. Factual material and statistics may not get
across well, and dictating notes is almost out of the question. But it can be a marvelous place for discussion, and
values seem to come across well in such an arrangement.
You plan the questions you want to ask, most beginning

with the word *why*. You keep your mind working to stay ahead and to keep the discussion moving. Jesus sometimes taught at the table.

Some classrooms have boardroom tables, and small groups can meet around them. These too can help us to cut through the structured situation and encourage learning. True, some teachers can use such a room for dictating notes, but that is not the room's fault. Again, a coffee urn can help encourage discussion. Some might object that coffee or soft drinks are a breach of classroom decorum. Some would object that such informality breaks down the formality of the teaching environment. Exactly. Someone might even spill his drink or leave his dirty cup on the table. But those are small prices to pay for encouraging a situation in which learning might take place.

It was in the informal situations that Jesus dropped memorable bits of instruction that made disciples out of His followers. By seizing on just such informal situations we can hope to drop the remarks that will lodge so deeply in our students' thinking. After all, what do we best remember of what we got from our teachers? Whole lessons or pointed sentences? How then can we plant those little time bombs that our students might remember?

TEACH OUTSIDE OF CLASS

To be sure, we have to make the best possible use of our time in class. Who would suppose that during one of Jesus' synagogue discourses anyone went to sleep? But since the gospels leave us not one account of Jesus' instructing His disciples in formal situations, we may do well to learn from His pattern. The disciples did hear Him in synagogues, on the hillsides, and from Peter's boat, but their real training seems to have come on the way to or from His discourses, or in the house, or at the table. Not that we automatically get disciples from such contact, but we will certainly not make disciples without such contact.

Each of us finds his own way. One opens his home,

and before long it becomes an unofficial student retreat. Another uses his office as a discipling place, with comfortable chairs, a coffeepot, and some mugs. Others make use of lunch rooms and coffee shops, using the opportunity for personal conversation. Pastors take students along to preaching appointments, and the car becomes a classroom. At least one former pastor of mine did that regularly, and I wonder how many Christian workers out there still look back gratefully to those trips, rich with instruction and fellowship, when each felt that he was the most privileged learner in the world.

A missionary told me that on the field he would often take a van-load of students on weekend deputations. They would talk and eat along the way. He would then drop off two-man teams at different villages on the way to his own preaching appointment. Sunday evening he would pick up his teams, head back to school, and hear the accounts of how their services went. His lasting impression was that such trips accomplished some of his most valuable work as a missionary. That's easy to believe.

Some might object that this sort of involvement costs time and energy. True enough, but what ministries are more important than training disciples? It costs to be a parent, and it costs to be a teacher. If we want to reproduce ourselves spiritually, there is a price we will have to count —and pay.

Some pastors feel frustrated at the slow growth of their Sunday schools or at the discouraging payoffs of their bus ministries. They might give thought to the quality of the teaching that goes on in the classes. How many of the teachers are up to the task? How many are doing little better than reading aloud from the quarterly and yearning for the closing bell?

If a pastor finds himself with such a teaching staff, he should consider discipling his teachers. He might have trouble blocking out a time when most could attend a training class, but in my experience many teachers welcome the opportunity. It is their chance to get some training in the lesson and to discuss ideas on how to make it vivid. Since many Sunday schools use the same lesson passage from junior high on up, one teacher training class can help most of the teachers. Such a class can pay off handsomely in enthusiasm, in quality of learning, and in numbers.

KNOW THE MATERIAL

In His supernatural knowledge and power, Jesus carried out His whole ministry according to a plan. In teaching His disciples He drew on the wisdom by which He had created all things. But few of His brief statements gave out information. He mainly imparted His values, often in warnings and exhortations. It may comfort us to note that those values are teaching resources we can draw on and can in turn share with our students.

To share those values we first have to learn them ourselves. Our daily time in Bible study counts here. A ministry of Bible teaching requires earnest preparation. Reflection on Scripture gives added dimension to its truth, and our response should be obedience. Anything short of obedience means that we are just playing with religion, and our students will not need long to interpret that message. A consistent obedience to the Bible will not only accredit our teaching; it will become a means by which we teach (Acts 20:26-35).

Is that to say that only the sinless ought to teach? Let us say rather that only the redeemed should teach. The qualified teacher confesses his faults to God, claims the cleansing blood, and admits his wrong to any people he may offend. He values the price of his redemption and of his forgiveness. For him is is all real.

The teacher who tries to live with nothing to hide in one sense has it easy. He has no great fear that his next remark will negate his ministry. In fact, even his off-hand remarks to his students will have teaching value. He becomes a living statement of the values of Christ. Any earnest student seeking answers to life's questions will find some of those answers just by being close.

COMMENT ON THE SCENE

Jesus made some of His most memorable statements commenting on the momentary situation. For example, the seventy came back from their preaching tour excited that even the demons had been subject to them. Jesus said, "I beheld Satan as lightning fall from heaven. Behold, I give unto you power to tread on serpents and scorpions, and over all the power of the enemy: and nothing shall by any means hurt you. Notwithstanding in this rejoice not, that the spirits are subject unto you; but rather rejoice, because your names are written in heaven" (Luke 10:17-20). In other words, no boasting about your ministry; be glad that you're saved at all.

Or the time that the rich young ruler, heavy at heart, was walking away. Jesus said to His disciples, "Verily I say unto you, That a rich man shall hardly enter into the kingdom of heaven. And again I say unto you, It is easier for a camel to go through the eye of a needle, than for a rich man to enter into the kingdom of God" (Matthew 19:23-24).

That shocked them.

Another example took place a day or so after His triumphal entry into Jerusalem. Jesus was sitting with His disciples across from the Temple. While they watched, people came to give money to the Temple treasury, some of them with conspicuous generosity. Jesus then quietly drew attention to a widow in the act of dropping in two tiny coins: "Of a truth I say unto you, that this poor widow hath cast in more than they all: For all these have of their abundance cast in unto the offerings of God: but she of her penury hath cast in all the living that she had" (Luke 21:3-4).

Even the casual remarks we may drop can convey values and meanings. Just as we trust our discourses to have their cumulative effect, we can work to use our casual remarks. Some may instruct. Some may express approval or disapproval of something. Some may give encouragement. And some of them will be long remembered.

How often did Jesus hold discipling sessions, concentrating His attention on one learner at a time? He may well have worked that way, but it is hard to find even one clear-cut case in the gospels. Nicodemus? John 3 looks more like evangelism. The woman at the well? Same story. The call of Levi? It says only that Levi followed Him. Zacchaeus? Individual attention, yes, but again it looks more like evangelism than discipling. Did Jesus spend quality time concentrating on Peter? He may have, but the gospels do not record that. Jesus did give him rebukes and encouragements but almost always in the presence of the others. The matter of the tribute money and catching the first fish to come up might be taken as an exception to that, but it appears to be only a brief exchange, not a prolongued discipling session.

What does that observation mean to us? Should we refuse to give individual instruction in discipleship? Most of us would hate to insist on that extreme; but as with other matters, such as our classrooms, our devices, and our agencies, let us at least remember the emphasis in the gospel records that Jesus did His recorded discipling in small groups and in informal settings. We may suppose that He discipled His men individually, but we have surprisingly few Bible verses to prove it.

Questions for Discussion

1. What sorts of learning best happen in a formal setting? What sorts best happen in an informal, unstructured one?
2. What are your own means for structuring your classroom so that learning can take place?
3. To what extent can you plan what you want to achieve in casual contact with your students? How do you plan

the informal contacts? To what extent do these contacts just happen?

4. What examples can you recall of getting values from your teachers or pastors? Sort those examples out into structured and unstructured situations.

8

Repeating Lessons

But they understood not that saying, and were afraid to ask him.

—Mark 9:32

Some teachers were sitting around talking about term papers and quality standards for research. One teacher argued that the school's students should have no problems writing good papers. His reason was that he regularly covered that material in a lecture delivered to all sophomores.

Do we not all share his wish, perhaps with less confidence, that students are learning material the very first time we present it to them?

It is a comfort to trace this problem in the gospels. If any teacher could get his material across the first time, surely our Lord Jesus could. Then we consider the number of times that He found it necessary to repeat His teachings, and we can take heart. The human mind does not often grasp ideas it hears for the first time. So if the Lord patiently repeated lessons, it is no surprise that we must repeat some of ours.

Sometimes we repeat material simply because it is important or because we are presenting it to different groups. Jesus repeated several of the parables for those reasons, notably the sower, the mustard seed, and the leaven. He used many of the ideas of the Sermon on the Mount in His discourse on the plain (Luke 6). Similarly we will repeat lessons to successive groups. One lesson we can draw, however, is that Jesus did not repeat the material in the same form in which He had given it before. Both discourses were fresh. If we have occasion to repeat material that we have already taught, we should follow His pattern by rethinking and reworking the lesson until it is fresh.

Even if we are drawing on years of experience, our material needs to be reworked until it is fresh again. Two preachers were talking about preaching old sermon outlines out of the barrel. One of them had strong feelings against the practice. The other protested, "But when you shoot a deer, you don't throw the gun away."

"That's right," countered the first, "but you do reload your ammunition."

One of the most common complaints about experienced teachers is that their courses have not changed in years.

But sometimes we have to repeat lessons to the same people we have already instructed, for various reasons.

Lessons That Did Not Get Across

The feeding of the five thousand provides an example of a lesson that did not get across. In Mark's gospel the sequence of events goes like this:

1. Jesus heard the report about the disciples' preaching tour and suggested that they withdraw into the desert to get some rest.
2. A huge crowd tracked Him out to the desert.
3. Jesus, moved with compassion, spent most of the day teaching the crowd.
4. Toward sunset the disciples broke through and urged Him to send the crowd away to get food for themselves.
5. Jesus said, "Give ye them to eat." He ended up multiplying the loaves and fish. Then before He dismissed the crowd He compelled His disciples to

get into the boat and start across. Soon the wind picked up, and they fought it through the night.

6. Toward morning, walking on the water, He came to the disciples. He then stilled the storm instantly.

Mark sums it up by saying, "For they considered not the miracle of the loaves for their heart was hardened."

That can mean only that Jesus was in the process of teaching them something that they did not learn:

1. He is sovereign over nature.
2. He reserves the right to demand the humanly impossible.
3. He meets our needs.
4. In tough situations we are to seek Him.
5. He has a compassionate heart for human needs, at the very time that He seems unconcerned about those needs
6. He loves His own, both crowds and disciples.

Whatever else He was doing when He was feeding the five thousand, He was teaching at least those things.

Apparently the twelve took it all for granted and missed the whole point of their experience. But note that when Jesus repeated the lesson, He repeated it in a different form. If they didn't understand the first time through in the desert, they could learn it during that frustrating night on the Sea of Galilee.

Thought question: As you compare the feeding of the five thousand and the stilling of the tempest, how many elements do the two experiences have in common? What pattern does that suggest for the next time you present material to your class and they fail to comprehend it?

The challenge is to present the same elements by as many different means as possible. Often our impulse in such a case is to repeat the lesson in the same words that we used before, hoping that speaking slower and louder will put the lesson across. A face or two may light up when we try it that way, but the majority will need a fresh approach.

But what about the relaxation that Jesus had offered the twelve? In all fairness, how much can we promise our disciples in the course of testing them? The directors of a certain mission candidate school promised all week long that a picnic was coming up on Saturday. Then Saturday they announced that there would be a work day instead. They wanted to see how the candidates would react to the change in plans. Most of us would call that dirty dealing. Was Jesus open to the same charge? I don't think so. It takes no great faith to suppose that while He ministered in Capernaum, the disciples had plenty of time to catch their breath—that Jesus did not trick them.

A second case of a repeated lesson that did not seem to get across was Jesus' rebuke of the Pharisees, material that appears in Matthew 12, 15, 23, Mark 7, Luke 11, 15, 16, and in other brief portions. He repeated that material partly because He was confronting different groups of Pharisees but also because He was teaching men who were steeling themselves against His words. It would seem that His words generated conviction but little repentance. When we try to instruct those who hate us, we can expect little more success than Jesus had.

A third lesson that did not get across was His prediction of the cross and of His resurrection. Some nine times in Matthew's gospel alone we have Jesus' predictions of His coming death, predictions made before the ones He gave during the Last Supper. Why their inability to understand? Because the truth was too momentous for them.

You and I with our New Testament understanding of prophecy could easily point to Psalm 22 and Isaiah 53 to show them things they already knew but had not fit together. For them, however, it was another matter. They knew that David's Son lives forever. They knew the predictions of Messiah's power. But of Messiah's suffering, Mary of Bethany was probably the only one who understood it.

Of the material that we have to get across, some kinds just do not soak in easily. Try explaining the balance between divine sovereignty and human responsibility. Try explaining the passage in Hebrews 9 on the death of the testator. Try explaining the Greek participles, and see how many class periods you need to get a quorum to grasp them. Try to explain submitting to every ordinance of man for the Lord's sake. In those cases, simple repetition is unlikely to convey the material. We search to find alternate ways to repeat the lesson in the hope that it will sink in: different words, different illustrations, different projects.

Lessons That Barely Got Across

Some of the lessons that we teach may get into our students' minds but not get in very deep. Some truths do not seem true to the flesh or to human pride. The subject came up among the disciples as to who was the greatest in their group (Mark 9:33-37). Jesus would have had to pry the admission out of them. Then with the little child in His arms He went over the principles of humility and service. We would think that the twelve would never forget.

In the next chapter Jesus has to teach it over again. James and John asked to sit next to Him in His kingdom, and the others were burning over their effrontery. So in different and stronger words Jesus went over it again: "But so shall it not be among you: but whosoever will be great among you, shall be your minister, and whosoever of you will be the chiefest, shall be servant of all. For even the Son of Man came not to be ministered unto, but to minister, and to give His life a ransom for many" (Mark 10:43-45).

A striking example of repeating a lesson appears in Luke 15. The Pharisees and scribes were grumbling at the social class of Jesus' converts. Jesus answered them with a parable, the parable of the lost sheep, and He concluded it with the shepherd's joy at finding it. He then recast the same story, this time in the form of the lost coin. As with the lost sheep, He made a point of the owner's joy at finding what he had lost. Then He gave the story in a third form, this time of the lost son, and He added a mass of detail and emotional appeal with which they could identify. Even before He got to the angry brother, the third form of the story had many times the impact that the first had had.

As we teach the Bible, human nature will resist some of what the Bible says. We accept that resistance; it is bound to come up in the teaching encounter, and we refuse to let it annoy us. We accept it as a challenge to find a way to repeat the lesson in such a way that our students will learn it.

If human nature can interrupt the flow of our teaching process, so does our students' cultural baggage. For example, the Bible has little good to say about collecting usury. Yet for the last three centuries some Christians have cheerfully collected exorbitant interest on the grounds that it is good stewardship. We do not have to go out of our way to challenge our culture's practices and notions. Soon enough, however, the Bible will contradict some commonly-accepted notion, and we can count on resistance to our teaching. Be prepared to repeat the lesson.

LESSONS THAT NEED REVIEW

Some lessons of their own nature fade easily, and we will need to repeat them. We live the spiritual life as aliens in a world that tolerates us. Our citizenship is in heaven. But not all our students think heaven's thoughts, cherish heaven's values, or speak with heaven's accent. Earth's music dins in their ears, and earth's advertising crowds into their vision. No wonder the gospels recorded so much of Jesus' teaching on the spiritual life. Much of the unique material in Luke 11-17 elaborates the spiritual life that Jesus had already taught.

Our students need to hear certain lessons reviewed. One of those is the cluster of doctrines connected with their salvation. Many Christians admit to a lack of assurance of salvation, and almost all cases of that will be found to go with someone's failure to ground them in the theology of what happened when they were saved. Listening to evangelistic sermons does not seem to make up for that failure in teaching.

Another lesson that they need often is the reminder to deal promptly with sin. "If we confess our sins, he is faithful and just to forgive us our sins, and to cleanse us from all unrighteousness" (1 John 1:9). Much of fellowship with God, dealing with guilt, and growth in grace turns on that simple requirement. Yet how easily the believer can ignore that principle and run up long accounts with God.

And when will we finally learn to worship? When will we become perfect in love? When will we finally and unerringly show Christian grace? When will we learn gratitude? When will we in all situations trust God? When will we finally quit being anxious? When will lust cease to tempt us? All of those are priorities that we need to repeat, first to our own souls and then to our students.

How did Jesus review, and how do we follow His patterns? As this chapter suggests, He repeated material, and we can class some of that repetition as review. Notice, however, that He did not review by simply repeating what He had taught before. When He repeated parables, such as the mustard seed and the leaven in Luke 13, He repeated them in different settings with different implications. When He repeated material from the Sermon on the Mount, He altered the phrasings, added new ideas, and omitted others that He might have repeated. We follow His pattern by reviewing from a fresh angle. We teach the same principle but in a different setting, in different words, or from a different starting point.

"Therefore we ought to give the more earnest heed to the things which we have heard, lest at any time we should let them slip" (Hebrews 2:1). God holds our students accountable to review what they have learned. We as teachers can at least try to make it easier for them.

Questions for Discussion

1. You are teaching a Sunday school lesson about the cross. You have stressed that Christ bore all the wrath that we deserve; and while God may chasten us, He does not punish us in wrath. You have used discussion groups, but you are not sure that the idea has lodged. By what different approaches might you review the matter?
2. In what specific ways did Jesus alter His lessons when He repeated them?
3. What means can we use to overcome our students' natural resistance to unfamiliar ideas?
4. How many different ways can you think of to review a given lesson?
5. What portion of class time should we spend reviewing?

9

Commendations and Rebukes

And Jesus answered and said unto him, Blessed art thou, Simon Barjona.

—Matthew 16:17*a*

If our disciples—our students—are to strive to learn, they need to enjoy some successes at learning. They will measure some of this success by the praise and encouragement we give them.

We feed their satisfaction by our approval, and our approval counts for something. In the long view, we do not want our students to remain dependent on us; we succeed when they become thinkers, leaders, and expositors in their own right. But in the early weeks and months we forge that temporary bond of trust, affection, and gratitude that teaching rightly involves. Later on, the bond of dependence will loosen and fall away. Our disciples break free, become independent, and in many cases surpass our own achievements. However, their affection and gratitude have a way of lasting indefinitely.

A writer was reminiscing about a professor he once had, a professor so exacting that we might call him a tyrant. Yet his classes almost always ended with intense discussion, and when he expressed approval of some student's arguments, the writer said it was like receiving knighthood. Quite a description.

What pattern can we find in the way that Jesus taught? For one thing, we do not find a trace of flattery; but we do find a series of encouragements and commendations for the believing, and we find a series of rebukes for the unbelieving. We can learn from both of those series. It seems self-evident that we should encourage our students and praise their successes. Why not? And what could be more elementary than that we should warn them against error and rebuke their unbeliefs? Yet if we omit either of those, we damage the learning process; and there is reason to believe that many of us are all too sparing in the encouragements we give out.

DEALING WITH CROWDS

"Blessed are ye, when men shall revile you. . . . Ye are the salt of the earth. . . . Ye are the light of the world" (Matthew 5:11-14).

As Jesus spoke to the crowds, He cared about them. Twelve times the synoptic gospels mention that He was moved with compassion, usually toward the crowds. That concern energized His discourses, in which He both encouraged and rebuked His hearers. In His sermon in Luke 6, He opens by four times pronouncing His hearers blessed and then follows up with four woes. He praised some impulses, but He also threw in the word *hypocrite*. All the way through, these discourses breathe warmth, optimism, concern, and encouragement. It is as if the very tone conveyed hope to sinners, at the same time that He was warning them against religious presumption. We find here no cool detachment, no hint of take-it-or-leave-it. Even the townspeople in Nazareth had marveled at the words of grace that came from His mouth (Luke 4:22).

As we teach groups, we follow Jesus' pattern by using both our words and our manner to encourage. We exude optimism; our very smile tells them that they have what it takes to learn what we are teaching. If sometimes the price seems high, it is not too high for them to pay. Though some of the material may be obscure, they can still come to understand it. Though the language be tonal or highly inflected, they can still learn to speak it. And when they succeed, we can reinforce their success with our praise.

Our experience will bear out what studies have shown. Divide a large class into three average groups, and set them to work on the same extended project. Praise the first group for the fantastic work that they are doing, and encourage them to surpass it. Scold the second group for the poor and inaccurate work that they are doing, and tell them you hope for better. Tell the third group nothing. Of the three groups, which one will probably do the best work? (If you chose group 1, you are right, of course.)

How do we use Jesus' rebukes? Many of us hate to rebuke people, and to rebuke a group in anger will probably turn them off permanently. Even short of anger, when we preach against sin we tend to dampen the spirit of the meeting. Teachers have told us to preach positively, but that was advice that Jesus did not originate or follow. He spoke out against sin, against unbelief, and against faked godliness. We too have to head off evil. If our hearers are going down wrong paths, we have to warn them.

Are we willing to address people as hypocrites? Jesus did it in two ways. When He addressed crowds, He spoke to wrong impulses among them, and in a general way He said something like, "Thou hypocrite, first cast out the beam out of thine own eye" (Matthew 7:5). That way He did not sting any one individual too deeply, despite His emphatic language. On the other hand, when He faced outrageous conduct in some individual, such as the synagogue ruler in Luke 13, He addressed him as a hypocrite; but that is a matter I will take up later.

Why should we encourage our classes? Well, we want them to succeed, don't we?

DEALING WITH BELIEVERS

To the believing, Jesus gave many encouragements. Jesus caught Peter fishing (Luke 5:1-11) and used his boat to teach the crowd. Then He gave Peter the first miraculous catch of fish. Peter threw himself at Jesus' knees and pled for Him to abandon him. "And Jesus said unto Simon, Fear not; from henceforth thou shalt catch men" (Luke 5:10). Jesus commended the centurion in Capernaum, and He encouraged the paralyzed man. He comforted the woman he had healed of the hemorrhage, and He encouraged desperate Jairus. He comforted the disciples in the boat and after rescuing Peter gave him only a gentle rebuke. He put off the Syrophoenician woman momentarily and then praised her faith. He commended Peter for his great confession, even though a few moments later he rebuked him for rejecting the message of the cross.

He also commended the woman in Simon's house, the seventy after their preaching tour, Mary of Bethany, the grateful cleansed leper, Zacchaeus, the poor widow (though not where she could hear Him), and the scribe who answered Him wisely (Mark 12:34). He was gentle with the woman taken in adultery, and He tried to encourage Martha. He was gentle with Mary Magdalene and with Thomas. Some of His last words to Peter encouraged him that he would be faithful to the death.

We may find ourselves marveling at how far our encouragements may lift our students. Some of them have already been battered by well-meaning parents and teachers. I knew a bright fifth-grader who could barely read. As his parents were discussing his problem, it occurred to them that they had often told him how dumb he was. In fact, they had probably not let a week go by without reviewing to him that information. At length he believed them and rested on what they had so often told him. As soon as they began finding other words to correct him and new words to encourage him, his classroom work began to improve. How many of our students could tell almost the same story? And how many of them could achieve kingdoms if only someone would give them a timely encouragement?

"For neither at any time used we flattering words, as ye know. . . . But we were gentle among you. . . . So being affectionately desirous of you, we were willing to have imparted unto you, not the gospel of God only, but also our own souls, because ye were dear unto us" (1 Thessalonians 2:5-8).

As we love our students, it should be easy to watch their progress, to commend their successes, and to encourage them when they fail. Jesus did not give up on us.

How many of us can trace our achievements to specific encouragements that others have given us? Would we not agree that an A in a tough course had only a fraction of the impact that we got from the moment some trusted friend or teacher commended us and told us that we could make it?

As I write this, I think of the way that such encouragements have led to ministries, enterprises, graduate degrees, and even marriages. How many ministries opened out when someone showed some encouragement? I think of three homemakers who earned B.A. degrees—and enormous satisfaction—because someone assured them that they could do it. Two of them now hold masters degrees as well.

On the other hand, what do we do when one of our students takes a wrong path?

The rich young ruler took a wrong path, and the Lord made no attempt to chase him, grab his shoulders, and plead with him to reconsider. In fact, we look in vain for His love to do that to anybody. Jesus loved the young man, but He just watched him walk away. When our prospective disciples harden themselves against the way of the cross, and we discern their hardness, we may likewise grieve in silence and let them go. Some of them may eventually reconsider.

What of true disciples who take a wrong path? In their case we must not fail to warn them. In such cases Jesus brought His disciples up short. Three times He challenged their little faith: to the disciples in the boat, facing death (Matthew 8:26), to Peter after he had walked on the water (Matthew 14:31), and again to the disciples in the boat after they had failed to grasp spiritual truth (Matthew 16:8).

When Peter rejected the prediction that Messiah would suffer, Jesus hammered him: "Get thee behind me, Satan: thou art an offense unto me: for thou savourest not the things that be of God, but those that be of men" (Matthew 16:23).

A week later the disciples tried and failed to cast out a demon. After Jesus cast it out, the disciples asked Him why they couldn't do it. He first pointed out their lack of faith and then explained that this was a particularly difficult kind.

A chapter later Peter was asking Him about the limits on the command to forgive—until seven times? Jesus did not exactly rebuke him, but His answer had force: "Seventy times seven."

When people brought little children for the Lord to lay His hands on and pray over, He rebuked His disciples publicly. Since our own experience will bear out how crushing a public rebuke can be, that gives an idea of how much Jesus valued little children. It also suggests that with our own disciples, the offense must be serious indeed to warrant our calling them down in the presence of outsiders—if that is what the gospels actually record. We would probably agree that the general rule goes for us, that in the presence of outsiders we back our students as far as possible, and we stand against them only when their conduct is indefensible. Otherwise we rebuke them only in private, and we will see that sort of loyalty breed loyalty.

In any case, we cannot let our disciples blunder on indefinitely doing what's wrong. We are duty bound to do what Jesus did: to rebuke their unbelief, to caution them against their sins, and to tell them what they should have done. Even in a climate of loving concern we may dislike having to correct them; but our concern should at least draw the sting out of the correction.

DEALING WITH UNBELIEVERS

Several instructive occasions give us Jesus' response to unbelief and rebellion. For example, Mark 1:40-45 tells us about the pleading leper and gives details that Matthew and Luke omit. The leper fell down at Jesus' knees and told Him that if only He wanted to, He had the power to cleanse him. Jesus, moved with compassion, touched the man and pronounced him clean. Instantly the leprosy was gone. Then Jesus' manner changed. Sternly, even angrily, He commanded the man to speak to no one, but to show himself to the priest and to offer the prescribed sacrifice. Then He sent him away. Little wonder if the translations barely convey Jesus' anger—how uncharacteristic of Him! But in the face of the man's unbelief and disobedience, we have to call such a rebuke Christlike.

Or consider the two blind men in Matthew 9:27-31. First Jesus ignored them, perhaps halfway across Capernaum. After they followed Him into the house, He finally asked if they believed that He had power to heal them. "Yes, Lord." Then with reserve He told them that according to their faith it would be to them; and as He touched their eyes, they received sight. At that moment He sternly rebuked them and told them not to tell anyone what He had done for them. Why the anger that time? Perhaps the only answer that fits is that healing was all that they wanted. They seemed destitute of any spiritual hunger. Jesus gave them only what they wanted, because they wanted nothing more from Him. So He rebuked them with anger.

He poured out His strongest rebukes on the men of the religious establishment. Events proved that most of those men had gone beyond repentance. They were men with scruples about Sabbath observance but who could plot the murder of an innocent man on the Sabbath day; men so devoid of spiritual discernment that they detested the one truly righteous man they ever met. Upon those men Jesus pronounced exposure and woe.

He rebuked the synagogue ruler mentioned in Luke 13. Here Jesus healed a woman who had been bent double for the past eighteen years, a victim of some sort of satanic activity. At that the ruler of the synagogue blazed with anger and complained to the congregation. It was probably the nearest he could come to religious fervor at what seemed to him such a desecration of the Sabbath.

Now if it were your move, what would you do?

"Thou hypocrite, doth not each one of you on the sabbath loose his ox or his ass from the stall, and lead him away to watering? And ought not this woman, being a daughter of Abraham, whom Satan hath bound, lo, these eighteen years, be loosed from this bond on the sabbath day?" (Luke 13:15-16).

He rebuked the Pharisees, as in the whole of Matthew 23, but not to induce them to repent; they were past that point. So why bother?

He rebuked the Pharisees because their evils cried out for rebuke. The prophets rebuked the evils of their days, and preachers used to preach against evils of all sorts. We speak against evils because they cry out for rebuke.

Jesus rebuked the Pharisees in the presence of the crowds and of His disciples. He used those rebukes as a way to minister to His own, to define evil and to warn against it. The disciples caught the idea. As we rebuke injustice, oppression, and fakery, we can hope to make our disciples sensitive to sins that they might not yet be tempted to commit.

As teachers we have the power to induce learning or to inhibit it. That power flows from the respect and the affection that bind teacher and student. That power can work through our approvals and our disapprovals, through our encouragements and our rebukes. On balance, the approvals and encouragements seem to accomplish more. Let us lay them on with zest.

Questions for Discussion

1. To induce learning, does praise really work any better than scolding?
2. How does our expectation of excellence bear on our students' actual performance?
3. How much or how little did Jesus praise His disciples? What different kinds of statements would have had the effect of encouraging them?
4. Regarding the value of commendations and rebukes, how much does grading bear upon a student's learning?
5. How has another person's praise or encouragement brought about a turning point in your life?
6. How many lives have changed direction because of some particular encouragement you remember giving?

10

Making Disciples

So likewise, whosoever he be of you that forsaketh not all that he hath, he cannot be my disciple.
—Luke 14:33

The goal of our teaching is to make disciples. To make disciples we must make demands. A veteran missionary was explaining his success in planting several churches: "We have not been afraid to make demands on our converts." Nor was Jesus.

The question we face is how many such demands we may rightly put upon our disciples. Many of us live with the desire not to put other people to any trouble, and if we want a job done right, we prefer to do it ourselves. Why be obtrusive? Why be a bother? Is it not more Christlike to do favors than to ask for them, to give rather than to receive?

Well, not always.

Many have observed that Jesus did not do for people what they could do for themselves. He turned the water into wine, but others had to do the pouring. He healed the paralytic, but others had gone to the work of lowering him down into Jesus' presence. The disciples prepared the Last Supper; only then did Jesus serve the food. He did wash their feet that night, but that was no exception when we consider what a powerful teaching device He made it.

It is not that Jesus was too proud to do menial work: "I am among you as he that serveth" (Luke 22:27). So may none of us become too proud to sweep floors, hang up other people's coats, carry bedpans, or clean toilets. On the other hand, Acts 6 requires us to delegate just about everything that someone else could do, while we give ourselves to what they cannot do or do not do. To the apostles that meant that they spent themselves in the ministry of the Word and prayer.

As we consider Jesus' demands, it must strike us that His claims are absolute. Jesus made many and sometimes heavy demands on His disciples, and we are going to have to repeat some of those demands. In making those demands, we know that in Christ we find no selfish motive; His demands were for the disciples' own eternal good. What is more, He demanded commitments no heavier than those He made upon Himself.

CALL THEM TO DISCIPLESHIP

"Follow me, and I will make you fishers of men" (Matthew 4:19).

"Ye are my friends, if ye do whatsoever I command you" (John 15:14).

The first demand that we make is our call to a potential disciple, and sooner or later we have to tell him what he is in for.

"If any man will come after me, let him deny himself, and take up his cross daily, and follow me. For whosoever will save his life shall lose it: but whosoever will lose his life for my sake, the same shall save it. For what is a man advantaged, if he shall gain the whole world, and lose himself, or be cast away? For whosoever shall be ashamed of me and of my words, of him shall the Son of man be ashamed, when he shall come in his own glory, and in his Father's, and of the holy angels" (Luke 9:23-26).

By the time that Jesus said that, the twelve had been preaching and healing for most of two years.

Whenever and however we do it, we are duty bound to tell our disciples, our students, what following Christ involves. Christ takes priority over family claims. To follow

Him is to drag the cross that we expect to die upon. To follow Him is to renounce all claims to pride, to things, indeed to any will of our own.

Paul the apostle accepted those terms for himself. He repeatedly called himself the slave of Jesus Christ. In addition, he taught those claims to his converts. To the first churches that he gathered he gave warning that through much tribulation they must enter the kingdom of God.

PUT THEM TO WORK

From the beginning of Jesus' ministry, He began calling disciples to follow Him (Matthew 4:18-22), and He seems to have taken them along on His preaching tours right away. John 4:2 implies that from the beginning of those tours Jesus had His disciples do the baptizing. Not long afterward Jesus spent a night in prayer and then called the twelve (Luke 6:12-16). Then some weeks or months later He sent them out to do what He had been doing (Matthew 9:35—10:42).

Note the order in which He did it:

1. He preached and healed, permitting them to watch His ministry (9:35).
2. He let them perceive the compassion that He felt toward the crowds (9:36).
3. He commanded them to pray earnestly for workers (9:38).
4. He gave them authority to cast out demons and to heal (10:1).
5. He gave them a whole chapter of specific instruction and encouragements.
6. He sent them out to serve.

Now, how do you follow that same pattern?

First, get some disciples and take them along to watch your ministry. You're already pastoring a church? Then it will be easier. You are a missionary preaching at various points? Take some promising men along. You are a teacher or a youth leader? Get several preaching engagements and take some of your students along.

Second, find ways to convey to them your honest concern for people. If we have anything in our hearts that regards people as sheep to be shorn of money or meals, we need to get that right before God, or we will damage the men we seek to train. They will surely grasp our insincerity. Worse, they might embrace our attitude as normal for themselves. If we genuinely care about the people we preach to, that care will get across to our students as the norm they are to live by.

Third, remind them of the believer's authority over the powers of darkness (James 4:7; 1 Peter 5:9). Nowhere in Scripture did God withdraw that authority of ours, which we use by the name and the blood of the Lord Jesus Christ. We must realize that we do not have authority over disease, however (Acts 28:28; 2 Timothy 4:20).

Fourth, after giving your disciples a chance to watch you at work, you should instruct them as to what their service involves. Go over some contingencies and prepare them for trouble. Assure them of God's jealous care over them. Warn them of the family disagreements that are likely to beset them. Remind them of the eternal rewards for serving Christ.

Finally, send them out to do the sort of ministry they watched you do.

How much should you monitor their work? Jesus seems not to have critiqued their preaching or healing, nor did He ever have them do any practice preaching; from the beginning their service was in real life situations. From the beginning He expected actual service.

We do well to follow the same pattern of reality service. In training our disciples, at no point are we to have them play parts, fill roles, or put on performances. Even in class we can insist on reality, or else we can send our workers to find reality on the outside.

TEACH THEM TO PRAY

From the beginning Jesus taught His disciples to pray. Only a few weeks after He first called them, they heard Him teach the Sermon on the Mount. Halfway through it He taught the basics of prayer: simple, trusting language to a loving Father, in secret, forgiving others in light of the forgiveness we have received (Matthew 6:5-15). He was teaching them to look to Him, and He concluded that period of His ministry by commanding them to pray—to plead—for laborers (Matthew 9:38). Jesus' teaching makes no requirement for skill, only diligence.

How do we apply those steps? Clearly by giving to our students the instructions that the Lord gave us: we teach them to pray directly to the Father, in simple and intimate language, with forgiveness for any wrong they may have suffered.

Some months later Jesus' disciples were ready for more. After watching Him pray, one of them asked Him to teach them to pray (Luke 11:1). Not *how* to pray; it is unlikely he had forgotten Matthew 6. He was now asking Him how to *go on* praying, how to spend time in prayer.

So how do we handle phase two? We follow Jesus' example by first reviewing what He had already taught them, the pattern of the so-called Lord's Prayer. Next we explain the principle of importunity, that if by returning again and again we can get answers from another person, how much more God the Father is going to respond to our continued coming.

Jesus' last instructions turned out to the disciples' final exam on prayer. After the Last Supper He led them to the Garden of Gethsemane. There, with events impending that they could not imagine, He commanded that while He prayed they should stay awake and pray. Jesus then agonized in prayer, and the eleven went off to sleep. Jesus woke Peter and asked if he did not have the strength to pray for an hour. What could he answer? Then Jesus gave them a startling command—that if necessary, they should pray standing up, lest they enter into temptation (Luke 22:46).

Sadly, they all failed the final examination.

Do we really need to teach our students to pray? We cannot very well leave that duty to others. It is all too easy to assume that our students are already praying. Or we may believe that the subject is too personal to intrude upon. However, if teaching prayer is an intrusion, we may need to go ahead and intrude.

If we can teach the urgency and the sweetness of vital prayer, we will bring blessing on our students' lives and ministries. If we fail to teach that urgency we will convey the alternate message, that contact with God is not particularly important, and service in the flesh is a live option.

But Jesus demanded that His disciples pray.

GET THEM TO GROW UP SPIRITUALLY

A further demand that Jesus made on His disciples was that they walk in spiritual maturity. Part of that maturity involved getting them to understand.

From early in His ministry He pressed them to think and to understand from God's point of view. He wanted His disciples to be reflective. Nowhere did He encourage pride of intellect; yet constantly He wanted them to think. We do well to challenge our students to think, especially in a religious culture that values activity but looks askance on reflection.

Our disciples need all the wisdom they can get. In recent days, the message of the cross has been reduced to a form of show business, and few seem to have noticed the loss. An easy religion has replaced the hard way of the prophets and martyrs, and the servants of the gospel have found ways to labor in affluence and comfort. The old message calling for repentance has given way to a new message calling for self-fulfillment. If our ministries are to mean anything more than Lot's in Sodom, it will be as we and our disciples sort out those contradictions and purify our messages.

A second evidence of spiritual maturity was that the disciples should forgive their enemies. In the Sermon on the Mount Jesus teaches forgiveness as part of a person's prayer life. In Matthew 18 He gives half a chapter to the moral logic in forgiveness: God has already forgiven us so much that we simply must forgive one another. Then at Calvary Jesus forgave the men who had just nailed Him to the cross. If we want to do our students some spiritual good, we must urge this further demand on them, that they forgive.

That leads to a third evidence of spiritual maturity—that they love one another. "By this shall all men know that ye are my disciples, if ye have love one to another" (John 13:35). The vocabulary of love has lately become commonplace, but when the love of many has grown cold, the very lack of love cries out for us to teach it. We can expect our students to start out with confused ideas; love is widely believed to be something we fall into, like an inheritance or a puddle. It is either a sexual activity or an emotional attraction of persons with like values. On that understanding, how could Jesus command us to love one another?

We do our students a tremendous service when we explain to them what Jesus meant by love: love means purposing the good of another, at any cost to oneself, hoping for nothing in return. To command a person to feel some emotion borders on absurdity. On the other hand, it is reasonable to command him to purpose something, and it was spiritually reasonable for Jesus to command us to purpose one another's good. As we show that kind of love to our students, we are qualified to teach. Such love accredits our testimony before the world; if we do not show it, the world has the right to judge us phonies. Such love makes lasting marriages and makes them wondrous. It holds churches together. It is the love that comes with spiritual maturity.

A fourth evidence of spiritual maturity is to accept the world's hatred. For nineteen centuries Christians have tried to find a middle way, to retain their identification with Christ, to preserve their claims on heaven, and at the same time to enjoy their ties with the system that crucified Christ. We must enable our students to find that fine line between love for souls ("for God so loved the world") and a love for the world system ("love not the world"). On one hand it is just good missionary work to meet the community leaders and let them know why we are in town. On the other hand, let us never hanker after the in-crowd, their parties, or their approval.

Our task is to find ways to strengthen our students, even to toughen them. John remarked at the number of top men who privately believed in Jesus but who, for fear of the Pharisees, refused to confess Him, so as not to be put out of the synagogue. "For they loved the praise of men more than the praise of God" (John 12:42-43). We don't want to produce that kind. As we stress the reality of the unseen world, as we stress the Lord's rightful claims on us, as we show our own example of devotion, we can hope to firm up our disciples toward the world and its enmity. Privately, we brace ourselves for some failures—Jesus did not give up on the apostles when they fled. But at the same time that we urge our students to be kind toward one another, tenderhearted, we work to strengthen them against pressures.

TEACH THEM RELIANCE ON THE SPIRIT

Jesus' teachings on the Holy Spirit come in three steps. First He planted the suggestion that they pray for the Spirit's working (Luke 11:13). As elsewhere in the New Testament, the passage does not suggest praying for the Spirit's indwelling presence but for the evidence of His presence. We must convey to our students the need for the Holy Spirit's power in their service, and, according to that verse, such power comes after prayer for it.

The second step in Jesus' teaching was His series of promises that the Spirit was about to come and work in the disciples. In John 7:37-39 He promises rivers of living water. In 14:16-17 He promises that the Comforter will indwell them and never leave. In 14:26 He promises that the Spirit will teach them and recall Jesus' words to them. In 15:26 He again promises that the Comforter will testify of Him. In 16:7-11 He says that the Comforter will have a convicting ministry and that ministry will begin after His coming to the disciples. Our experience will bear out that He mediates much of that convicting through the believers, whom He indwells.

We impress these promises on our disciples: that they can hope for the rivers, that they can count on the Spirit's eternal indwelling, that He will remind them of Christ, and that through their ministries He will convict the world of sin, righteousness, and judgment.

The third step in Jesus' teaching on the Spirit was to command the disciples to appropriate the Holy Spirit's power. The imperative in John 20:22 implies all this and more: "Receive ye the Holy Ghost."

REMIND THEM OF CHRIST'S CLAIMS

Although it is true that our justification rests on faith alone, Christ bade us be His disciples. His claims of discipleship become absolute demands.

In practice, not every believer becomes clear on that idea. For years mission executives have echoed what a leader once remarked, "We get an inquirer, and the first question he asks is about our retirement program." A missionary candidate who rated more than two dozen conservative boards finally chose one on the ground that its support level was almost three times the average of the others. After twenty-five years in a large church, one pastor's salary and allowances came to more than three times the total missions budget of the church.

What a contrast to Jesus' requests of Peter in John 21! Jesus had risen from the dead. Peter had gone back to fishing. But after a whole night of catching nothing, he had to face Jesus, who questioned him on three subjects and said in essence:

1. Love. "Do you love me more than these? Do you love me? Do you like me?"
2. Service. "Feed my lambs. Tend my sheep. Feed my sheep (no more fishing)."
3. Death. "When you grow old you will still be faithful. Your death will glorify God."

We have moved beyond legalisms and prohibitions to the ultimate questions:

1. Do you love Jesus Christ? How much do you purpose His happiness? Do you love Him enough to do what He commands you to do? Do you love Him enough to spend quality time with Him daily?
2. Do you purpose to serve Christ? Does He have free course to fix the terms of your service? Have you signed a blank contract for Him to fill out? Have you accepted the possibility that He may ignore your wishes, even as you trust Him for your own ultimate good? If He should choose it, do you consent to menial work? Will you consider foreign missions as a real possibility for your life work? Are you willing to accept the principle of living off your ministry?
3. Do you purpose to serve Jesus Christ to the death? Do you purpose that by His grace even the threat of death will not break your testimony of faith in Him? Do you purpose to serve Him, even if at last it should be to die alone or to go to an unmarked grave?

As we deal with our own students, these may be the final demands that we lay on them. By whatever means we can we need to motivate our disciples to make these concerns their own. Short of pressing these claims, we may do some instructing, but we will not be teaching as Jesus taught.

11

The Teacher's Commitment

*And whosoever will be chief among you, let him be
your servant: Even as the Son of man came not to be
ministered unto, but to minister, and to give his life a
ransom for many.*

—Matthew 20:27-28

It was true of Christ, and it should be true of us, that we
believe in both the truth and the value of what we teach.
Those of us who teach Bible should have no difficulty with
that; let us trust that each one of us loves the Book. But
what of those other subjects that we may find ourselves
teaching? Even here we gain something when we satisfy
our minds that we do value them.

Even more important than our commitment as
spokesmen for truth is our worthiness as life models.
Chapter 1 made the point that we should prepare to teach,
not just by mastering the material in a given teaching field,
but by preparing ourselves as men and women after whom
our students can model their lives. Our presence becomes
a sort of teaching device, a means by which we show what
we are conveying. What we are then actually speaks so
loudly that our students can hear what we say.

This chapter bears down on those who teach as Christians in whatever situation. The Christian teacher of indus-
trial arts in a secular situation has different pressures from

those of the missionary teaching Bible to fresh converts. In the secular situation the Christian has only a relative commitment to his subject matter; in five years the textbook may change radically and the course itself become obsolete. But the fitness of things demands that he be no less a Christian than the missionary.

Question for thought: How much Scripture could we find to defend this last statement?

If teaching rightly demands of a believer that his body should go on the altar forever, what does our Lord's example tell us about that commitment?

VALUES

Jesus held certain values, certain commitments. Some of those He held because He was God. For example, He had no conscience of sin. He knew that He was Messiah. He knew that He would one day judge the world. He knew those things about Himself; He did not have to clutch at deity. We have no way to share such mysteries as those.

Jesus held certain other values that we can share, such as His love for His Father. We have already looked at His practice of prayer, of worship, and of obedience to the Father. His meat was to do the will of Him who sent Him. We take it as an article of faith that He loved the Father. That love was an eternal bond that we can barely comprehend, yet He bids us share it. "As the Father hath loved me, so have I loved you: continue ye in my love" (John 15:9). When the disciples asked Him why they could not cast that demon out, His reply carried a weight of meaning: "Because of your unbelief. . . . This kind goeth not out but by prayer and fasting" (Matthew 17:20-21). He was offering them the hope of the power that was constantly His; all that they had to do was spend time in prayer. Their determination to get through to the Father was to mean more to them than their meals.

We can have it if we want.

"He that hath my commandments, and keepeth them, he it is that loveth me: and he that loveth me shall be loved of my Father, and I will love him, and will manifest myself to him" (John 14:21).

He invites us to the inner circle.

Jesus also valued the Scripture as the immediate message from His Father. He used Scripture in the moment of temptation. He drew on Scripture both as His teaching source and as His authority. He obeyed Scripture as the expression of His Father's wish, even as He was fulfilling the prophecies and types of Himself. He made Scripture His comfort on the cross, and He taught it to His two disciples on the Emmaus road.

In a corresponding way we value the Bible. We treasure its verses. We love its binding and pages, not as an object of worship but as the bearer of God's verbally inspired message to us. We cling to the Bible in temptation. We teach it as the substance of what we convey, and we draw our authority from it. We believe its promises, and we attempt to do what it tells us to do. We remember it in our sufferings, and we rest on it in our anxieties. And finally we hold its truths as we die, trusting God for the resurrection. We do not live by bread alone.

What is more, Jesus valued truth and right. In a culture where truth is relative and moral values weak, murder has become merely unsportsmanlike; adultery is often only a poor option; and lying just tends to undermine trust. Stealing is an annoyance to the loser and a challenge to the defense counsel. Killing a baby sounds more tidy if it is called termination of pregnancy. Yet Jesus stood against such clevernesses.

To follow Christ is to collide with Western thought. He would have none of our relativism. Rather than justify murder, He condemned even the source of it. Rather than justify adultery, He condemned even easy divorce. Rather than justify innovative sex, He condemned lust. Rather than justify lying, He condemned showy prayers as dishonest. He condemned theft in any connection, and, far from justifying abortion, He invited little children to come to Him.

If we follow Jesus Christ, Scripture binds us to truth and right as absolutes. God is our rock. But was Jesus not moved with compassion toward sinners? True, but He did not condone sin; nor did He authorize us to condone what God views with revulsion. He forgave the woman taken in adultery, but He did not give her His permission to go on committing it. He told her to quit doing it any longer; He did not use the word *compassion* to authorize the practice of lechery.

To follow Christ is to follow the One who twice cleansed the Temple and who looked with anger on religious phonies. The zeal of God's house ate Him up. Yet He was not judgmental with Levi or Zacchaeus.

Jesus valued love, but the sort of love that overcomes sin. He loved His own, and He loved those who refused to be His own. He commanded His own to love one another. He was moved with compassion at the multitudes and those who were suffering. He wept over the city of Jerusalem. He was a friend to tax-collecting outcasts and to sinners. At the last He forgave those who crucified Him.

To follow Christ means to accept the love principle, to confess our failures, and to make ourselves care about others. To follow Christ is to attempt to feel with His compassion or to yearn that we could. To follow Christ is to accept a holy altruism, spending ourselves for others and putting their interests before our own. In terms of a teacher's life, it means being glad to take phone calls at odd hours, so as to clear up obscurities left over from a lecture. It means to rejoice at the promotions of our fellow teachers. It means to be willing to counsel and to encourage at one o'clock in the morning, rejoicing with those who rejoice and weeping with those who weep. To follow Christ is to learn to grieve over hard hearts.

CONSISTENCY

Of the divine qualities we see in the Lord Jesus, a striking one is His consistency. First to last He taught a constant message. We can believe that if He had ever negated it, no one would have written a gospel about Him. "Jesus Christ the same yesterday, and today, and for ever" (Hebrews 13:8). He was always unthreatened, unshockable, controlled, and holy. His anger never contradicted His love; His forgiveness never contradicted His righteousness. He did always those things that pleased His Father, and He never betrayed the trust that He had merited from the twelve.

This purity, this consistency, we owe to our teaching task. When we contradict our own instructions, we either corrupt or we devastate our students. One foul word, one lie, one flash of selfishness, and we blow our credit. Even to contradict our teaching will hurt our credibility, as when the driver education teacher runs a stop sign, or when the professor of Christian ethics compromises himself in administrative campus politics. We discipline ourselves, keeping our bodies under and bringing them into subjection, lest we ourselves should be disqualified.

SACRIFICE

The proof of our commitment as teachers is in our willingness to sacrifice. It may take no commitment at all to read a lecture, to lead a discussion, or to demonstrate a process. To do any of those as a Christian requires only a bit more. To teach the Bible and to make disciples requires a great deal more; in fact to teach that way means to submit to ultimate demands. Our students have some right to ask of us what our teaching has cost us. What scars? What sacrifices?

We will need a better answer than that we do not like the pay.

To Christ, the beginning of sacrifice was entering this

world. And what an entrance: from the glories above, through the servants' entrance into the scullery. Then a life of poverty, misunderstanding, and contempt. At the beginning of His ministry He went through the water of baptism, the innocent taking the place of the guilty. After six weeks of fasting, He endured all that with which the devil could tempt Him. In the next years He had nowhere to lay His head. What is worse, His own received Him not, and the nation's leaders hated Him. Sacrifice indeed.

The night of the Last Supper Jesus laid aside His outer clothes and washed the feet of His disciples. He laid aside His pride, His self-image. He laid aside His leadership, as they understood it, and accepted the place of slave. It was one thing to create those feet; it was something else to wash them. If the disciples found it distasteful to accept such service, let us put ourselves in the Lord's place as He rendered it. By contrast, how undemanding to prepare our messages and deliver them. Are we at least willing to wash our students' feet? Because based on Jesus' pattern, teaching may cost.

At His trial Jesus stood alone. John was not far away. Peter was near the fire, until he vanished with the others. Alone Jesus faced His inquisitors. It was not only as Teacher that He endured the mock trials, the flogging, the scorn, and the cross. Yet through all those agonies He never negated the message that He had taught. He suffered as our sacrifice, but He also suffered as our Teacher, sealing with His blood His commitment to the truth He had given us.

In the Western world we have long been free from physical persecution. We have little idea of how the cell, the whip, or the bullet can test our will to follow Christ, although some know what it is to be hated for His sake. Even the peer pressure against us is nothing like that which Russian Christians face daily.

Does Jesus expect His disciples to make the same life-and-death commitment that He made? After He put the three love questions to Peter, He assured Peter that he would remain faithful to Him to the death. Thereupon Peter asked Him about John. Jesus' answer seemed to avoid the question, but it still implied that John, like Peter, would live out that same final resolve.

Frail though we may be, we still owe it all to Christ. We are not playing games. Whether pioneering a field or leading a home Bible study, whether teaching a throng or a tiny class, we hear the martyrs' call. They do not call us to suffer for methods or techniques. They call us to value the truths that we teach and the Christ who saved us. To those truths and to this Lord we commit ourselves with unflinching purpose.

IN CLOSING

People have found ways to remind me that we can't all be pastors, missionaries, or teachers. After all, God does not call everyone, nor does He give those gifts to all believers. Furthermore, we need a strong financial base for the Lord's work, and Bible teachers are not the sort to provide it. Of course, that line of thought is correct, at least so far as it does not rationalize someone's refusal to go as a missionary.

If we cannot all be preachers and teachers, almost all of us can find ways to give the Word of God to others. Some of us may live off that ministry; many of us do not. If God has called us to live off a Bible ministry or vocational Christian service, we had better yield quietly. If He has not laid such a mandate upon us, we still try to keep our lives at His disposal and then sleep with an easy conscience. We can continue to seek ways to give His Word to others. What Sunday school teacher would not be glad to be the Edward Kimball who led D. L. Moody to Christ? You can't get a Sunday school class? Could you organize a home Bible study? You can't face a group? Can you find ways to speak to individuals?

Because whatever way we can find to do it, what can be more satisfying than to give God's Word to others? I look back over more than three decades of Christian service, mostly as a teacher, and marvel at the high privilege of such a life. We should find high motives to teach: love for Christ, love for others, duty, aspiration. It is a form of selfishness to serve Christ for the satisfaction we may get out of it. But for us who teach, what satisfactions! We have the privilege of looking back, not just to old lecture notes and old yearbooks, but to lives changed, lost people saved, ministries launched, and families blessed. We can identify workers whose ministries have surpassed ours, workers in whom we can yet discern the mark we once left upon them. We can see people brought to Christ by our former students, people we could never have won ourselves. We can reflect on churches built, schools aided, and mission fields entered, works in which God has enabled us to have some indirect influence.

What more could we ask?

"And Jesus answered and said, Verily I say unto you, There is no man that hath left house, or brethren, or sisters, or father, or mother, or wife, or children, or lands, for my sake, and the gospel's, but he shall receive an hundredfold now in this time, houses, and brethren, and sisters, and mothers, and children, and lands, with persecutions; and in the world to come, eternal life" (Mark 10:29-30).

May the Lord bless your teaching.

Moody Press, a ministry of the Moody Bible Institute, is designed for education, evangelization, and edification. If we may assist you in knowing more about Christ and the Christian life, please write us without obligation: Moody Press, c/o MLM, Chicago, Illinois 60610.